The Wisdom of
Groundhog Day

The Wisdom of Groundhog Day:

HOW TO IMPROVE YOUR LIFE ONE DAY AT A TIME

Paul Hannam

yellow
kite

First published in Great Britain in 2016 by Yellow Kite
An imprint of Hodder & Stoughton
An Hachette UK company

First published in paperback in 2017

1

A CIP catalogue record for this title is available from the British Library

Paperback ISBN 978 1 473 61920 3
eBook ISBN 978 1 473 61918 0

Typeset in Sabon MT by Palimpsest Book Production Ltd, Falkirk, Stirlingshire

Printed and bound in Great Britain by Clays Ltd, St Ives plc

Hodder & Stoughton policy is to use papers that are natural,
renewable and recyclable products and made from wood grown in
sustainable forests. The logging and manufacturing processes are expected
to conform to the environmental regulations of the country of origin.

Yellow Kite
Hodder & Stoughton Ltd
Carmelite House
50 Victoria Embankment
London EC4Y 0DZ

www.yellowkitebooks.co.uk
www.hodder.co.uk

To two wonderful women.
My mother, Mary, and my aunt Terry.

contents

foreword

It still delights and amazes me that *Groundhog Day* (1993) is still enjoying such a great, long life. Over the years people have developed what I can only describe as a personal relationship with this movie about a weatherman stuck in an endlessly repeating day.

I know this about people because they tell me so, and the letters and stories have been remarkable. The first fan mail I ever got was from a monk in Germany.

A monk.

In Germany.

After that came a note from a young couple who studied the Kabbalah, a practice of Jewish mysticism, and there was one from a professor of philosophy in Pennsylvania who had a bet with his students that I had based the movie on Nietzsche's theory of eternal recurrence. I've gotten mail from psychologists who prescribed the movie to their patients; from Buddhists, who voted it the best Buddhist movie ever; from cancer patients who told me they watched the movie and found inspiration and healing.

Director Harold Ramis was receiving the same kind of mail and the two of us were sheepishly giddy about it, yet delighted. Our movie was being seen and talked about. People were getting from the film a lot of what we had intended, and that alone was gratifying; but beyond that we were being sent serious scholarly works, articles from professional journals, and even sermons. This was not your usual fan mail.

It seems that something about the movie had tapped into a common human experience that had finally found a common language. In fact, 'Groundhog Day' is now so commonly used as an expression that it has literally entered the lexicon.

Let me be clear: none of this was intentional. I was writing a movie that I thought would be clever, funny, fun and interesting – the kind of movie I most enjoy both writing and watching. It would have comedy and tragedy, romance and excitement, and with luck I would be able to sell it. I was not trying to tell a morality tale or a religious parable, not trying to teach, preach or educate. Harold and I had some great conversations about reincarnation and rebirth, the moral responsibility of being Superman, the psychology of dying and similar subjects – we were clearly aware that there were resonances with these things – but our focus in making the movie was just to tell Phil's story, and tell it as truthfully as we could.

That being said, the original inspiration for the movie was more than a 'man-repeats-day' comedy concept. It began, in fact, with a musing about immortality. I was wondering: would a person stuck in his adolescence ever grow out of it, even if he lived for ever, or would he always remain stuck no matter how long he lived? This thought intrigued me, but 'eternity' felt like an awfully long time for a ninety-minute movie. Plus they'd have to build a lot of sets.

Then I had a thought: what if this epic journey took place on one single repeating day?

In the next split second I knew that this was a good idea. By combining eternity with repetition I had stumbled onto a very strong vehicle for comic ideas, characters, themes and storyline. And what we all discovered on the other side of this process was *Groundhog Day*.

It is a little bit intimidating to be introducing a book that includes 'wisdom' in the title. The way I think about wisdom is that it isn't wise unless you've found some use for it – so it's always about the relationship between the so-called 'wisdom' and your own life. For example, you might think that 'Look before you leap' is a wise thing to live by when your kid is chasing a ball into the street; but 'He who hesitates is lost' might be the thing that gets the kid through the deer in-the-headlights situation that almost follows. My point is, first of all, the kid is fine. The other point is that even though I'm honestly humbled by any association with the goodness found in this movie, it's always going to be up to you to figure out what to do with it. And this book, The Wisdom of Groundhog Day, may help give you some ideas on how to do just that.

Paul Hannam is a wonderful teacher and business entrepreneur who has succeeded in connecting people with fulfilling work, big ideas and big causes. And if anyone can help you see this movie from new angles and find even deeper connections, it's him. I hope you enjoy the process.

Danny Rubin

DANNY RUBIN continues to teach and speak about screenwriting, most recently as the Briggs Copland lecturer on screenwriting at Harvard (2008–13). He is currently working on several new screenplays; on a paperback version of his popular eBook *How to Write Groundhog Day* and on a musical production of *Groundhog Day* scheduled to open in London in 2016 and on Broadway in March 2017.

the time of your life

No matter what happens tomorrow, or for the rest of my life, I'm happy now . . .

Phil Connors, *Groundhog Day*

What if I were to tell you that you already have everything you need to be happy today, tomorrow and for the rest of your life? That you can improve the quality of your moment-to-moment experience significantly, whenever you want, wherever you are, whoever you are with and whatever you are doing. And that you don't need more money, status or achievements to do this. All you need is to unlock the natural resources that you already possess.

And what if I were to tell you that you can find the key in an unexpected place: in the film *Groundhog Day*? This deceptively simple comedy delivers a life-changing lesson in how to turn a terrible day into a wonderful one. I call this the wisdom of *Groundhog Day*, and it will help you to lead a life full of joy and fulfilment whatever your circumstances.

1

With its intense focus on one day in a small town, *Groundhog Day* celebrates the extraordinary gift of ordinary life: it helps you to appreciate simple pleasures that you may have previously taken for granted; it affirms your amazing, innate capacity for happiness, which you may have lost sight of; and it highlights those remarkable natural resources such as resilience and resourcefulness, which you may formerly have ignored. Above all, it lays out a clear path for making better choices, getting out of a rut and creating a brighter future.

On the one hand, *Groundhog Day* is science fiction – a fantasy about being trapped for ever in the same recurring day. Yet at a deeper level, it presents a compelling, timeless vision of how to live in the real world. It offers powerful strategies for the same universal challenges that we all face: how to deal with setbacks, rejection and loss; how to handle boredom, uncertainty and disappointment; and how to manage change, power and intimacy. Whether they are negative or positive experiences, we all manage them differently and it is clear that some people do so better than others. The question is whether there is an ideal approach to working through life's great challenges – one that is available to all of us.

Groundhog Day suggests that there might well be, through understanding the transformation of the main character, Phil Connors, a cynical, ambitious TV weatherman. Over the course of the film, Phil has the opportunity to test and evaluate a limitless number of different approaches to managing universal challenges. He shows us the way forward by proving that if you are agile, resourceful and tough you will succeed.

He demonstrates that if you keep on experimenting, you will eventually find the most rewarding way to live each day to the full. And we can all do the same. We can discover a practical wisdom that will help us expertly navigate the hazards, detours and wrong turns we all experience, and also ensure that we enjoy and appreciate every moment of the journey.

This is the exciting promise of *Groundhog Day*, and watching the film again and again over the years has changed my life in many positive ways. I have attained two degrees, read innumerable books, notched up over thirty years' experience in applied psychology, attended and run over two hundred personal-development workshops, trained many thousands of people, built large businesses and taught at Oxford University, and yet I still turn to *Groundhog Day* for inspiration and guidance on how to be happy and fulfilled. In my view, it is the greatest story ever told, and I want to share its wisdom with you – because I know that understanding and applying this wisdom can help you change your life for the better too.

Groundhog Day is a tale about how Phil Connors becomes trapped in the small town of Punxsutawney, reliving the exact same day, 2 February, over and over again. Eventually, he escapes the time loop, but only after he has completed a life-changing journey of self-discovery and transformation.

While he is stuck in the loop for years, maybe decades, Phil has to struggle with what seems like a devastating fate. He is stuck in time. Nothing changes – not the town, its inhabitants or events; not even time. The same people perform the same activities and speak the same words. Everything is static except Phil. Only he has the ability to change.

At first, he is in shock and denial. Then he manipulates the situation to serve his own interests, seducing women and committing crimes for fun. He is playing at life, but when the novelty wears off, he sinks into despair as he relives his nightmare over and over again until, on this never-ending freezing February day, Phil loses all hope and hits rock bottom. He wakes at 6 a.m., smashes his alarm clock on the floor and drags himself to work. Unshaven and unkempt, he delivers his despondent report to the camera, concluding: 'There is no way this winter is ever going to end.'

With dead eyes and a resigned voice, Phil tells his producer, Rita, 'I've come to the end of me,' and, with death seemingly the only way to stop his suffering, he tries to kill himself. He drives off a cliff, electrocutes himself with a toaster in his bath, walks in front of a truck and throws himself off a building. Yet he cannot die. He still wakes up the following morning to repeat the same day.

Then, slowly, something begins to change. He accepts that he cannot escape and prepares to face the reality of his predicament. After incalculable days of trying, he starts to turn his life around.

Phil learns – through perseverance, resilience and resource-fulness – to gradually adapt, cope, grow and, ultimately, triumph over adversity. He turns a bitter February day, when all hope seems lost, into a perfect day. He ends the film smartly dressed and cheerful. He delivers a heartfelt report to the camera, this time concluding with: '. . . standing here among the people of Punxsutawney and basking in the warmth of their hearths and hearts, I couldn't imagine a better fate than a long and lustrous winter.'

He is a reformed character, spending his day performing acts of kindness. He catches a boy who is falling from a tree, changes a tyre for some old ladies and saves an important local official from choking. That evening, at a town party, he entertains the crowds with his piano playing and is praised by the same people he used to despise. Rita says to him, 'You seem like the most popular person in town,' and, after she has outbid everyone at the auction to win a date with him, he sculpts her face in ice and they wake up together on a new day, 3 February. Phil has escaped the time trap and is free at last!

make every day amazing

There is a life-changing secret at the heart of the film: you can make every day amazing if you choose to. Phil learns how to transform the exact same day from the worst of his life into the best. And so can you! You don't need to be stuck in time like Phil. Nor do you need to move to a tropical paradise, win the lottery, become a celebrity or make any dramatic changes to your life. You can create your perfect day at home, in the office or wherever you are now.

The key is understanding exactly what alters between the worst day of Phil's life, when he tries to kill himself, and the best, when he is in a state of bliss and enlightenment, falling head over heels in love. This one unchanging day is both frustrating and fun, depressing and hopeful, dull and exciting. Time stands still, but Phil learns how to move forward.

Over time, through trial and error, Phil learns how to master the art of living this one day, his only day, to the full. By making small, ongoing advances each day in his thinking, attitudes and behaviour, he dramatically enhances the quality of his experience until he creates a perfect day. He improves by comparing different versions of himself from day to day, and experimenting with different ways of dealing with his predicament.

You can follow Phil's lead. You can learn and apply the exact process of self-improvement that he discovered in Punxsutawney. You also have the power to create the day you want, whenever you want. You can make today bright or gloomy, inspiring or dull. So why not choose to feel joy rather than boredom, hope rather than emptiness and love rather than self-absorption? The way you approach life and the way you interpret what happens to you have a profound effect. Every time you choose a bright day, you lay the foundations for a magnificent life.

No story better delivers the greatest lesson in life – that only you can make yourself happy and fulfilled. As Phil discovers, no one and nothing else is going to do that for you. Each scene contains clues, tools and practices that emphasise this critical point. Phil Connors learns that he has all the resources, and all the resourcefulness, he needs to survive and flourish. And while he has to relive the same day countless times to reach this realisation, you can get there in normal time.

I know this is true from my own experience. From my teens, I struggled to be happy. For many years, I suffered from anxiety and, at times, depression. I tried to deal with this by continually changing my circumstances in the hope that this would fix my problems. My strategies included starting new businesses, moving home, living abroad and relentlessly distracting myself from a pervasive feeling of emptiness. I was always searching for something or someone to fix me. I was looking outside of myself when the answers were always within.

I tried every possible treatment and tactic in my search for relief and, after years of false starts and wrong turnings, I discovered a way of life that has made me far happier. As I watched *Groundhog Day* again and again, I immersed myself in it, detecting a deeper meaning and significance in each scene. And I had an epiphany: I realised that this story about timelessness reveals timeless wisdom. It has taught me life-changing lessons that I want to share with you.

how to get the most from this book

When you have read this book and applied its insights and practices to your own life, you too will enjoy a greater sense of wellbeing, purpose and fulfilment. By fully engaging with the extraordinary quality of ordinary life, you will notice that each minute, each hour and each day feels better than before. And, as you become better able to handle whatever challenges life throws at you, you will be more resilient.

I have structured the book so as to provide a step-by-step process through which you can explore, understand and simu-late Phil's progress towards a fully engaged life. In Chapter One you will discover why *Groundhog Day* is such an extraor-dinary film, with a potentially life-changing message. Chapters Two and Three describe the Groundhog Day Condition that keeps you stuck in your 'Conditioned Self', determining your experience and enjoyment of life. You will see how you can accept and understand the limitations of your Conditioned Self, so that you can break free and prepare the ground for unconditional happiness.

In Chapters Four and Five, you will learn how to transcend and move beyond your Conditioned Self by living in the present and engaging with life directly. When he arrives in Punxsutawney Phil lives in his own head, and only becomes engaged when he begins to pay attention to what's happening around him. Once he became aware of the present moment and appreciates what he has, he is able to lay the foundations for genuine progress towards lasting joy.

Next, in Chapters Six and Seven, you will discover the power of engaging with yourself. Phil becomes self-aware, and finds meaning, purpose and his core values. He achieves this by activating the same capabilities, or natural resources, that all of us have, including the ability to experience joy and love at all times, to feel calm and to find meaning in everything we do and to be passionate, fulfilled, optimistic and resilient each and every day. Phil discovers these, as well as his own innate wisdom and sense of wellbeing. He engages with the best version of who he is, or his 'Authentic Self'. You have an Authentic Self too that you will uncover when you embark on your own voyage of self-discovery and self-improvement, and learn how to engage with your values and purpose.

The final stage of engagement is engaging with others. Phil overcomes his habitual cynicism and self-centeredness, and connects with the townspeople and the world around him. He learns how to be a member of the community, to build relationships and be a loving person. In so doing, he attains a level of joy and fulfilment that previously seemed un-imaginable. Chapter Eight will show you how you can do the same when you focus on putting other people first, and finding a purpose greater than your own self-interest.

I will then help you to integrate the wisdom of *Groundhog Day* into your daily life by introducing the concept of prac-tice in Chapter Nine – because to bring about a significant change and lead an authentic life, you will need to practise. Phil practises the art of living every day until he gets it right. There are thousands of self-help books, and many of them repeat the same ideas and messages – you may well have read some yourself, and have a good understanding of psychology and personal development. But my challenge to you is this: have you used that knowledge? Have you done the work? Have you improved your day-to-day experience through consistent practice?

My purpose is to help you adopt an experimental mindset, and to discover innovative ways to more successfully navigate the peaks and valleys of everyday life. Like Phil, you have the power to create your perfect day, each and every day. So, join me on a voyage of discovery. Follow the clear, proven route that is in front of you, and I will support you every step of the way. You can take this journey whoever you are, wherever you live and whatever life you are leading. You can enhance the quality of your everyday experience in days, weeks and months, rather than the decades it took Phil. February the second was Phil's time. Today is yours. You can become the best version of yourself today. And you can be happy now and for the rest of your life.

CHAPTER ONE

time for a change

What would you do if you were stuck in one place and every day was exactly the same and nothing that you did mattered?

Phil Connors, *Groundhog Day*

'Groundhog Day' has become a popular idiom to describe a feeling of déjà vu and repetition. But it also has a far deeper meaning. In the film, Phil is imprisoned in time. He is literally 'serving time' and this can describe life for many of us. We may be free in the literal sense of the word, but we don't live as though we are. Our lives are determined by routine, schedule, habit and the demands of others. Many of us are slaves to a lifestyle we have unwittingly created.

The film highlights how the repetitive nature of our everyday existence can imprison us, and it also reveals how we can escape. The time loop is a powerful catalyst for change, as it forces Phil to find answers to the great questions we all face: how do we find meaning? How do we find love? And how do we deal with fear and loss? Over the course of a lifetime, we will have to come up with our own answers, and the process is often complex, unclear and unsatisfying. Phil develops his own process by trial and error. He begins to observe his thoughts and feelings, and tries something new each day until he finds answers.

You too will find answers by learning from your direct experience, and observing the regular patterns of your own life. You develop in response to different people, different situations and events. Sometimes you look directly for answers in books, with mentors or even in therapy. But most of the time, your character is forged in an indirect, complex and dynamic interplay of relationships and influences that is largely outside your awareness until you pay attention to it. Phil unlocks his potential for joy and fulfilment by paying attention to every detail of his experience. So can you.

At first, you may find it hard to observe the subtle shifts in your inner life, as they occur almost imperceptibly, day by day. The ingenuity of the film is that everything is static. Nothing changes in the outside world, so we are able to focus on exactly what is happening to Phil, highlighting adjustments that are normally unnoticeable. We are compelled to see his life in sharp focus and in slow motion, so we can gain a much richer understanding. Phil is like a participant in a controlled scientific experiment. You can examine how he brings about change and see its effects close up. In his sealed-off world, his life is compressed into a single slice of time and place.

Over time, Phil begins to realise that change can only come from within. And the implications of this shift in mindset are both fascinating and significant. How will he develop and grow without normal external influences? Is there a growth pattern that unfolds naturally? Does he possess an innate wisdom that he will eventually discover and be guided by?

There is nowhere to hide in the time trap. Everything Phil thinks, says and does is held up to scrutiny repeatedly, and with scientific rigour. Every minute detail of his life is tested and evaluated, as each day is testament to either his success or failure at making progress. If you observed each day in such detail, you would become aware of what you actually do, not what you think you do. You would discern the governing patterns of your life and, perhaps, begin to appreciate the wisdom of *Groundhog Day*.

If you are ready to pay close attention to your daily experience, and evaluate your thoughts, feelings and behaviour, you too can achieve your own personal transformation, just like Phil. You should also be prepared for some surprising results. Once you shine a light on your character, lifestyle, beliefs, fears and aspirations, your strengths and your weaknesses will all be exposed. You will be able to experiment with, and measure, the effectiveness of new attitudes and behaviours just like Phil does. It will be demanding but exhilarating – and it will be life-changing.

a life in a day

Groundhog Day distils a lifetime into one recurring day, providing a unique frame of reference for understanding the whole span of a life in only twenty-four hours. You can see every emotion on display, from the depths of despair to ecstatic bliss.

You can also see Phil's character develop in the way he handles each repetitive day. As he changes his inner life, he changes his outer life. As he alters his mindset, his perception of Punxsutawney alters too. The town and its people reflect and affirm his level of progress, on his journey of personal growth. As he seeks to exploit people, he suffers. As he becomes more enlightened, he gets immediate, positive feedback from the town. He learns to deal with 'Instant Karma', to quote John Lennon.[1] *Groundhog Day* is instant karma in action: it magnifies the impact of everything Phil does by giving direct and immediate feedback, so he can evaluate the results of his actions. At first, his bad thoughts and deeds lead to anguish. By the end, his good, loving thoughts and deeds lead to joy.

In many ways, our outer lives are a reflection of our inner lives, but because we are so busy we rarely see how our moods and feelings create our own experience. We think we are happy because something good has happened, and sad because of something bad. We believe that the perfect outer life will give us the inner life we want – that owning the 'right' car or home will generate the feelings we desire. But the opposite is true: we need to create a positive inner life to attain the outer life we want. And this process becomes visible in *Groundhog Day*. Punxsutawney is a projection of Phil's state of mind: as he changes his inner life and warms to the town, the townspeople change and warm to him too.

Consider to what extent the state of your life is a projection of your state of mind. Does the quality of your relationships or your career reflect how you feel inside? If you want to feel different, then focus on changing your inner life rather than your outer life.

Write down how you would like to change your inner life? What would you like to feeling right now?

_____

_____

_____

_____

_____

_____

_____

_____

from here to eternity

The genius of *Groundhog Day* is that Phil not only has to confront the same dilemmas we all have to face, such as how to overcome loneliness, fear and loss, but that he has to face them again and again. Yet, through practice, he discovers a way in which he does not just cope with adversity, he genuinely flourishes. He learns something valuable from each failure. Every perceived loss leads to an unexpected gain as he learns to bounce back from each setback. The time loop proves to be the ultimate class in mastering the art of living.

You can follow Phil's example by thinking about how you would answer these questions:

- What would you change if you could only change yourself?
- How would you live if you could live for ever?
- Is there a way to be happy and fulfilled that works for everyone?

If you want to join this class, you can start by putting yourself in Phil's shoes and imagining how you would deal with immortality. As you do this, you may reconsider how you want to live the rest of your life. You may evaluate how you fill your time currently? What is the structure of your days?

The familiar routines and schedules of Phil's days are torn apart as time stands still. This begs some interesting questions. Who are you when this structure is removed, and you have no roles or responsibilities? How do you cope if you have no goals, no plans, no career or dreams? Do you feel this way sometimes? If so, then you should know that there is always hope, as Phil discovers when the familiar signposts of everyday life disappear and he has to find his way with no map or compass.

As you consider the nature of your inner self, you will hopefully become clearer about how you want to spend your invaluable time. You may re-evaluate how you spend it at home, and in your career, with greater awareness, respect and urgency. You might become more serious about being happy. You might even think anew about the point of your life and the legacy you want to leave behind.

Phil begins to understand what most of us already know in our hearts: a happy and fulfilling life is built on love not fear, on helping others not ourselves, on gratitude not craving, on being fully present and discovering purpose and meaning. The crucial question is why we fail to follow our hearts so much of the time.

You may intuitively sense that there is a better way to live. I am sure that you would rather be like Phil at the end of the film, than at the beginning. And deep down, you may realise that your challenge is not so much knowing what to do but actually doing it. Leading a good life is really quite simple. The skill is getting rid of all the obstacles that are in the way, and accepting that most of them were put there by you.

This is the essence of *Groundhog Day*. We keep on making the same mistakes day after day, and risk becoming trapped in an endless cycle that blocks our path to the bright future we yearn for.

This cycle of repetitive behaviours remains largely out of your awareness. It may be so ingrained that you mistake it for reality. You tell yourself that this is just the way life is and you stay stuck. I remember a client who remained in a loveless, stagnant marriage, but was in denial. Her parents' marriage was also unsatisfying, and she acted as though this was the inevitable fate of all couples. For years she justified her predicament and created a story of stoical perseverance that kept her stuck. She had surrendered her power of choice. She could not admit that she should get out, and instead did nothing. The cycle that she had unwittingly created was too strong.

The wisdom of *Groundhog Day* helps to make these invisible patterns more visible. Its fictional world projects and exposes the nature of the real world. By applying to your own life the original and creative perspective of rewinding time, you can better understand yourself and what will make you happy. Here are some examples of patterns that keep us stuck. Do any of them resonate with you?

- You want to start your own business, but don't want to take the risk of leaving a secure job.
- You want to end a relationship, but are anxious about the potential upheaval and how your friends might judge you.
- You want to live more simply and downsize, but you are worried about a loss of status, and that others will think you have financial troubles.

- You want to stop spending time with a group of old friends who are always negative and critical, but you don't want to upset them.
- You want to write a book, but you feel people will make fun of you and that you probably don't have the ability.

In identifying these or similar patterns you will gain a deeper understanding of what motivates you and how you may be creating your own version of *Groundhog Day*.

CHAPTER TWO

the groundhog day condition

We are all stuck in our own time trap. 'Groundhog Day' does not simply refer to the repetitions and routines in your outer life. It also explains the repetitive patterns in your inner life. Maybe you have the feeling of reliving the same day even if the place, people and events are different. As the French say, '*Plus ça change, plus c'est la même chose*' (the more things change, the more they stay the same).

I call this experience the Groundhog Day Condition. It is the feeling that things are out of your control and that you are disengaged. It is the sense that your life is repetitive and that you have the same thoughts and feelings most of the time. Locked into a continuous state of worrying, multi-tasking and busyness, you feel disconnected from the direct experience of life, from other people and from the real you. I suffer from this condition and so do millions of other people. It provides an explanation for how and why you feel the way you do, offering insight and a compelling answer to these questions:

- Why do you feel stuck?
- Why do you find change so hard?
- Why do you feel unfulfilled?
- Why do you feel that life is passing you by?
- Why does what you think you want often turn out to be disappointing when you get it?

The Groundhog Day Condition helps to describe and even help explain many chronic problems such as anxiety, stress, dissatisfaction, lack of meaning and loneliness. When you feel caught in an unrelenting cycle of commuting, working, paying the bills, collapsing in front of the TV, and sleeping, it highlights the question of whether this is how you want to live.

The condition is insidious. It is like a virus that you get used to, and then believe to be entirely normal and permanent. You may be unaware that you have the condition, or choose to ignore, deny or accept the symptoms. When you are locked into your own version of *Groundhog Day*, you are restless, busy and rushed, and anxious about what you should be doing next.

The condition affects all of us to different degrees. It is a side effect of our twenty-first century lifestyle, aggravated by our culture, circumstances and habits. It is the daily grind of endlessly repetitive tasks, tiresome encounters with the same people and meaningless activities. It is giving up on your dreams, good intentions that go nowhere and settling for a comfortable life. It is the feeling of loss – of life passing you by, of resignation and of missing out. Above all, it is the disconnection or disengagement from your experience of living, from other people and, most disturbingly, from yourself.

You may feel a general sense of dissatisfaction, or that you are just going through the motions. When Phil Connors visits a bowling alley and starts talking with two local drunks, he complains about his fate: 'What would you do', he asks them, 'if you were stuck in one place and every day was exactly the same and nothing that you did mattered?' One of the drunks sadly replies: 'That about sums it up for me.'

Does this sum it up for you? From working with thousands of people as a coach and trainer I can confirm that this is a common feeling. Moreover, few people understand how they end up feeling this way. The exact force that keeps Phil trapped in time is also a mystery; it is happening against his will and beyond his control.

I see *Groundhog Day* as a metaphor for the different forces that keep us all stuck. We are convinced that they are external, and that our unique circumstances are what's holding us back. We deceive ourselves into believing that they are beyond our control, like the weather. Yet the truth is that we have far more influence than we realise.

From my experience, the real culprits are the forces of habit, inertia, routine, negative thinking, our unconscious drives and anxiety. But above all, fear is the strongest force, and when you overcome your fears, you are far better able to make the choice you want, not the one you feel compelled to make. You are stronger than you realise, and have the ability to counter all of these forces, fear included.

what are the symptoms of the condition?

For years, I faced my own version of *Groundhog Day* every day. I would get up each morning and immediately fixate on what I had to do that day, on what was troubling me and what was missing in my life. It felt like there was an invisible force pushing me in a negative direction as soon as I was awake. Perhaps you fixate on a recurring challenge, such as dealing with workplace stress, a painful illness or a difficult relationship? Whatever your particular challenge, the condition is a distinctive phenomenon featuring a set of behaviours, thoughts and feelings that present themselves as at least one or more of the following five symptoms:

- The feeling that you are stuck
- Compulsive thoughts and feelings
- Living on autopilot
- A sense of meaninglessness
- Powerlessness to change

1: THE FEELING THAT YOU ARE STUCK
This is the primary symptom of the Groundhog Condition. We all get stuck; sometimes we are aware of it and sometimes we are not. At work you can get stuck in limiting habits like

avoiding risk; at home it can be damaging patterns like having the same weekly argument with your partner about money or housework. I am sure that you also have friends or acquaintances who have been stuck in unhappy marriages or jobs for years, paralysed by the burdens of guilt and obligation.

Phil's life is repetitive and most of us face the same predicament. While we might not be trapped in time, we may be entrenched in self-limiting patterns more than we would like to admit. Sometimes, it is a subtle sense of limitation, other times it can be an overwhelming feeling of oppression – of a great weight holding us down as if we are imprisoned by routine.

One of the best examples of this is found at work. I have trained and coached thousands of people over almost thirty years. I remember one manager at a bank who spent his whole week moving from one meeting to another. He felt he had no control over these meetings, and that he was reacting to other people's agendas and could never change his routine. He spent several hours explaining to me why he believed nothing could be done, as it would upset others and contradict policy and procedure. It took many months until he realised that he could alter his schedule. Eventually, he reduced the number of meetings he attended by half. This improved his outer life, but doing it meant that he had had to break free of his limiting, repetitive beliefs in his inner life too. This was the greatest reward of all. He liberated himself from his own Groundhog Day. Like him, so many of us know that we have free will, yet we continue to live as though we don't.

2: COMPULSIVE THOUGHTS AND FEELINGS

Phil makes lots of changes and tries many activities, but his thought patterns and emotions remain the same until near the end of the film. His mind is dominated by one compulsive, overriding thought: what's in it for me? He might be thinking about the potential bank robbery one day, getting drunk the following day or seducing Rita the next. The activities might be different, yet his intention remains fixed.

Do you struggle with recurring thoughts and feelings? You're not alone. For centuries, spiritual leaders and meditation experts have been teaching that our thinking is compulsive, and that rather than us choosing most of our thoughts, they happen to us.

It's not just that the thoughts are always arising and seem uncontrollable, but that they are frequently negative too – why am I so tired? Why did they get the job I wanted? I wish I could afford to retire. What is going to happen to my children? – and so on. If you wake up in the middle of night, you can be hit by a flood of these unwelcome visitors that seem impossible to resist.

Our thoughts create our reality, and, most of the time, our thinking is in reaction to what is happening to us. Phil is completely reactive when he arrives in Punxsutawney: he reacts negatively to the town, the people, the Groundhog Day ceremony and the weather. But it is not the freezing weather there that lowers his mood. It is the weather he brings with him. How about you? Do you bring sunshine or gloom with you into your home and office? I am as guilty as the next person but, as I watched the film again and again, I realised that I was creating my own storm clouds – and that I could blow them away too.

Our reactivity and compulsive thoughts are also reinforced by the stories we tell ourselves. *Groundhog Day* is a metaphor for how we retell the same stories in our minds and relive the same patterns. I created my own story after the crash of 2008 when I was living in California. As my environmental businesses collapsed, and the value of the house I lived in dropped by 30 per cent overnight, I blamed the economy, the government, society and various people too. It helped me feel better for a while, but I found myself repeating the blame cycle over and over, like a self-pitying drunk. Whoever I met, I would reel off my woeful tale, and the story became a part of my identity. I sounded like a stuck record, as I reconstructed again and again this unhappy period in my life, perpetuating my own misery.

We all have our own scripts and stories – about our parents, our education, our career, our families and our ups and downs – that shape our sense of self. But the question is this: is your story accurate, and, more importantly, does it serve you or not? Maybe it's time to create a new narrative that motivates you and gives you purpose, and to let go of the old stories that keep you stuck.

You cannot change the past, but you can change your interpretation of it. You can choose to focus on how your experience has made you more resilient, or you can choose to be a victim. You can create any story you want and each of them will be true for you. So why not choose one that will help you to be stronger, happier and more fulfilled?

3: LIVING ON AUTOPILOT

Phil is on autopilot when he arrives in Punxsutawney. He is not conscious of the town, the people or the festival. He is just going through the motions of his job to get out as quickly as possible. Do you do the same? Do you replay the same routines day in day out? Are you still following the well-trodden path that has been laid out for you since childhood – unquestioning, perhaps even unaware that there may be an alternative?

Conventional education, career, relationships and lifestyle provide a powerful map and structure for your daily life. For many this provides a degree of stability and order. But the flip side is that they may be sacrificing self-determination for security, spontaneity for structure and passion for passivity and a steady income.

How are your choices working for you? Is your struggle less about physical and more about emotional survival? Maybe this is the life you have settled for, not the one you want to be living. It is easy to become enmeshed in a pervasive 'activity trap' that can restrict your experience to a narrow spectrum of thoughts and emotions. You might reduce your anxieties and fears by staying constantly busy and distracted, but it is at a price. You resign yourself to a familiar, secure routine that numbs the pain, but also numbs your joy and passion. The Groundhog Day Condition contracts your experience to a habitual mindset that disconnects you from the full richness and abundance available to you.

Indeed, this universal dilemma has been recognised by modern social commentators, and also by various spiritual traditions. The Buddhist concept of *Samsara* means to wander around in circles; it is our fate until we learn to awaken.[2]

We generally spend our days in 'doing mode': we perform tasks on autopilot – habitual activities, such as planning the day ahead while driving to work. When we are fixed in this mode it is hard to shift to 'being mode', when we simply experience the immediate sights, sounds and feelings around us in the present moment. Sometimes it can feel like we are in a trance, hypnotised by the relentless pressures of everyday life. Have you ever felt this way? In a typical busy day, how conscious are you of your moment-to-moment experience? When you are driving, are you unconscious most of the time as everything is automatic? Compare driving today to when you were first learning. Then, every movement and action demanded intense concentration and deliberation. Today, they require no such attention, as you do them automatically. The problem is that so much of the rest of your life also becomes automatic through time pressures and force of habit.

Your day-to-day existence is directed largely by unconscious, recurrent behaviours, like the way you communicate, manage your time, make decisions and complete tasks. Here, for the most part, you are operating on autopilot. This unseen force takes you in a direction that largely determines the quality of your life. If you want to change, you have to discriminate between the habits that keep you stuck and those that will liberate you. Otherwise, you risk sleepwalking through life, disturbed by the nagging feeling that you are not living your life, but that life is living you.

> **So habitual is the trance of ordinary life that one could say that human beings are a race that sleeps and awakens, but does not awaken fully. Because half-awake is sufficient for the task we customarily do, few of us are aware of the dysfunction of our condition.**[3]
>
> Arthur J. Deikman, professor of psychiatry

4: A SENSE OF MEANINGLESSNESS

Phil loses all sense of meaning in the earlier stages of the time trap. Nothing he does seems to matter. In many ways, he suffers a mid-life crisis, a traumatic life transition made worse by the apparent futility of his unique plight. He is forced to turn his attention from making a living to making a meaningful life. A tough existence is bad enough; meaningless repetition is far worse. And a life without meaning, ultimately, turns out to be unrewarding and empty.

The Greeks had their own version of Groundhog Day: the Myth of Sisyphus. As a punishment from the Gods, Sisyphus is condemned 'to ceaselessly rolling a rock to the top of a mountain, whence the stone would fall back of its own weight.

They had thought with some reason that there is no more dreadful punishment than futile and hopeless labour.'[4]

More recently, during the Victorian era, British prisoners were put on treadmills to drive machinery. But when some of the prisoners found solace in doing useful work, the authorities disconnected the treadmill from the machinery, to make it a meaningless activity. This proved to be a worse punishment.

Do you sometimes feel that you are walking on a treadmill without purpose? Are you unsure of your reason to get up in the morning? If so, you have to figure out what motivates you at your core, and find a 'why' for your life beyond merely existing. For once you lose sight of the bigger picture, you risk losing direction and becoming a hostage to your own instincts and fears.

Many people feel disengaged, disenchanted and uninvolved, even when surrounded by family and friends. They view their jobs as draining and unrewarding. Long working hours, continuous stress, endless multitasking, the fear of unemployment and the absence of any work/life balance aggravate their sense of disengagement. For many, life may have lost its meaning.

In the course of my career, I have discovered that employee disengagement is a chronic problem. Numerous studies suggest that in countries such as the UK and US over half of the workforce feels disengaged, and many more suffer from 'presenteeism', which is just going through the motions.[5] It is a tragedy that such a large proportion of employees spend the majority of their adult lives working without meaning, purpose, creativity or passion. I have witnessed first-hand the damaging emotional cost of disengagement, as people leave their hearts and souls at home and treat work as a means to an end.

Disengagement is also destructive outside work as it saps your vitality. Do you feel restless, impatient and irritable? Do you have trouble sleeping? Do you feel bored and less able to enjoy former pleasures? All of these are signs that you are disengaged – that you feel detached from colleagues, friends and even family. It is as though you have lost your way, which can be debilitating. Without direction, you are vulnerable and liable to getting stuck in repetitive patterns of behaviour. Without meaning, you risk wandering aimlessly through life.

5: POWERLESSNESS TO CHANGE

Phil starts to believe that he does not have the power within him to change. The time trap represents an unseen deterministic force that places severe limits on his free will. Like a hardened addict, he feels he has no power over his destiny.

Do you feel locked into a way of life you are powerless to change? Do you say to yourself, 'Why do I keep doing this? I can't seem to stop.' Do you find it almost impossible to change? I often feel that I am not in charge of my mind or my actions. I feel compelled to complete tasks, meet deadlines and always be busy. I know I have a choice, but typically slip into what seem like pre-programmed steps in a choreographed performance. I stick to my script as I play my role without questioning whether or not I am in the right play.

In your encounters with others, you may also follow the same well-rehearsed scripts. You frequently say and do what you think you ought to, ignoring what you feel below all the surface noise. At work, this can be aggravated by organisational politics and an attempt to keep up appearances. The office can sometimes seem dehumanising, as you react to one challenge after another, trying to fit in and conform. Life can seem like a series of habitual reactions to an unchanging procession of people and events.

We all become set in our ways, feeling that our capabilities, beliefs and feelings are fixed and that we have little power to change them, or to change ourselves. This hinders our personal growth and is what Stanford psychologist Carol Dweck calls a 'fixed mindset'. She contrasts this state with a 'growth mindset' which embraces change, continuous learning and, of course, growth. Through my work with people over the last thirty years it has become clear to me that the vast majority are limited by a fixed mindset. Phil shifts from a fixed to a growth mindset and I urge you to do the same.[6]

If you feel entirely powerless to change, you may suffer from what psychologists call 'learned helplessness'.[7] This can creep up on you in subtle ways. You gradually adapt to your day-to-day experience and lose sight of your autonomy, and your innate ability to make choices. You start to have thoughts such as, 'This will never get better' and tell friends that 'There is nothing I can do.' Your language betrays an over-whelming sense of helplessness. You feel incapacitated and habituate to your lot in life.

In *Groundhog Day*, time is meaningless and it places the responsibility on Phil, as he can't fall back on the hope that things will change in time. There is nothing around the corner for him. The grass will never be greener. He has to take action and change himself or nothing will change.

So ask yourself if you genuinely want to change and get out of a rut? Could life be better? Above all, consider whether you are prepared to try something new and take a different approach so you can break free. If you are ready to take personal responsibility, regain your independence and live life on your own terms, there is a way forward right in front of you.

living in the age of anxiety

The five symptoms of the Groundhog Day Condition outlined above are exacerbated by social conditioning, especially by our consumer culture. We enjoy a much higher standard of living than ever before, but this has not led to a corresponding higher standard of feelings. In fact, if anything, material progress is diminishing our emotional experience in many ways.

We are working longer hours, and commuting further, to make more money to consume more things that we do not need and, crucially, that are not making us any happier. We have bought into a way of life whereby we are feeling too stressed, sleeping too little, being too sedentary and struggling to find fulfilment. Indeed, this lifestyle is making us more vulnerable to stress, anxiety and depression than ever before. We are connected to technology but disconnected from life. We seek shelter from a raging storm of discontent by plugging into our smartphones, tablets and laptops. And the emotional cost is devastating.

The Groundhog Day Condition shares characteristics with what Freud called 'free-floating anxiety',[8] and what is currently known as generalised anxiety.[9] This is a general sense of restlessness, frustration and discontent. It is the constant feeling that you should be doing something else, that you are not doing enough or even that *you* are not enough. It can also be a fear of missing out, otherwise known as FOMO. You think others are enjoying life more than you are, that something better is happening somewhere else, that you are not going to the best parties or visiting the coolest places.

At a deeper level, this is dissatisfaction with your life as it is, and a forlorn yearning for how life could or should be. The Buddhists call this *Dukkha*, the suffering of everyday life. You may be unaware that you are experiencing the condition as it is so insidious. Or maybe you have got so used to it you have forgotten what it is like to not feel tense and agitated. You may also know in your heart that this is not your destiny – that your potential is so much greater.

SUMMARY

• We all suffer to some extent from the Groundhog Day Condition – the feeling of being stuck in a rut or reliving the same day in our heads.

• The Groundhog Day Condition can help to describe and even explain many chronic problems such as anxiety, stress, dissatisfaction, lack of meaning and loneliness.

• There are five symptoms of the Groundhog Day Condition: the feeling that you are stuck; compulsive thoughts and feelings; living on autopilot; a sense of meaninglessness; powerlessness to change.

• The Groundhog Day Condition is made worse by our modern culture and media which contribute to our restlessness, anxiety and disengagement.

CHAPTER THREE

your conditioned self

'You are fettered,' said Scrooge, trembling. 'Tell me why?'
'I wear the chain I forged in life,' replied the Ghost.
'I made it link by link, and yard by yard; I girded it on of my own free will, and of my own free will I wore it.'[10]

Charles Dickens, *A Christmas Carol*

As we have seen, the Groundhog Day Condition might best be described as the invisible force directing your life through the unconscious agency of routine and habitual thinking. This creates your 'Conditioned Self': all the emotional, cognitive and behavioural chains you have made, link by link, both consciously and unconsciously since you were born. It is your recurring thoughts, feelings, attitudes, habits, values and behaviours. It is how you make sense of the world, and it is how you deal with everyday life.

Ultimately, it is your Conditioned Self that keeps you fixed in your own Groundhog Day, and prevents you from unlocking your potential. Rather than experiencing the world directly, you experience it through your Conditioned Self which creates its own distorted reality. This is your personal reality and it determines your current level of consciousness.

The force exerted by your Conditioned Self is similar to the mysterious time loop that keeps Phil trapped in repetitive cycles. He is locked in two prisons: the prison of time and the prison of his Conditioned Self. It takes him a very long time to understand that only by escaping from the latter can he escape from the former.

The primary function of your Conditioned Self is to protect you from emotional pain. It is, however, a Faustian pact – because in return for temporary relief and an illusory sense of security, you dull your emotions and restrict the development of your character. You stay confined in your familiar routine, reassured by a deceptive feeling of control while rarely feeling the extremes of sadness or joy. Unaddressed, an obsessive yearning for security can lead to stagnation. Fear curbs your development, and your emotional landscape is restricted to shades of grey, when there is a whole world of colour that you only glimpse occasionally. Fear of the unknown keeps you marooned, stopping you from venturing beyond the familiar and making you vulnerable to chronic anxiety. Fear of your potential outweighs your apprehension about being in a rut. In the words of author and spiritual teacher Marianne Williamson:

Our deepest fear is not that we are inadequate. Our deepest fear is that we are powerful beyond measure. It is our light, not our darkness that most frightens us.[11],[12]

But what triggers the Groundhog Day Condition, and what is the process by which we create our Conditioned Self? Let's look more closely at the three main causes, which are:

- your conditioning
- your circumstances
- your mind.

your conditioning

I am convinced that our conditioning from birth has a bigger impact than our personal situation on how our lives turn out.

Your conditioning is the set of influences on your life up to now, and includes your family, education, peer pressure, culture, social norms, technology and the economy. You interpret your circumstances through the lens of your conditioning. At the start of the film, Phil is very much the product of his fast-paced media career. He enters Punxsutawney with a sense of superiority and a cynical aloofness that prevents him from enjoying the town and its people.

Similarly, every moment of every day your conditioning

acts as a powerful filter that structures your experience. It creates repetitive patterns of thinking, feeling and behaviour that reinforce the Groundhog Day Condition, and tends to limit your passage through life to well-trodden paths.

In the West, this normally means a material path. We are raised to work hard, to achieve financial success and to consume as much as possible. Our schooling, parenting and most other aspects of our conditioning push us in this direction and it is very tough to change course.

This process is based on a number of shared assumptions and beliefs. The challenge is that you risk conflating them with your identity as they have become so deep-rooted, and seem as much a part of you as your age or gender. They normally reside at an unconscious level, though you may recognise one or more of them:

- I have to be in control.
- I need approval.
- I need to feel secure.
- I need more money.
- I must be right all the time.
- I am entitled to what I want.
- I must never make a mistake.
- Everything in life must be fair.
- Everything must go my way.
- I must be successful to be happy.

The strength of these beliefs means that powerful experiences can freeze you in a moment in time. In a second, you can revert to thinking, and feeling, like the insecure little boy or girl at the back of the classroom, when facing difficult people or challenges. This can drive your behaviour if left unchecked, but is not who you really are. You are who you are now, not a frozen self-image from years ago.

your circumstances

Your personal circumstances are the observable, measurable aspects of your life. As such, if I was to ask you what the problem with your life was, you would probably respond that your circumstances were to blame. Millions of people living in poverty are genuinely trapped by theirs. For you, however, the challenge may be less about your circumstances and more down to your expectations about improving them: if only you had more money, more time, a better job, a bigger house or a new partner, you would be just fine.

One of the biggest flaws in our thinking is our obsession with changing our circumstances, in the hope that this will make us feel better. When we get angry or feel miserable, our first impulse is often to think about what we need to do to fix this. We look to our work, our possessions, our relationships and other external features of our life for an answer, while completely overlooking the glaring truth that happiness comes from within. Phil learns that he cannot change anyone or anything other than himself. So maybe it is time for you too to stop devoting so much effort to trying to change your situation, so you can experience the feelings you want? Maybe it is time instead to discover that you can have those feelings right here, right now?

your mind

The third cause of the Groundhog Day Condition is the way your mind works and, in particular, its preference for habitual and automatic thinking. Even if, and when, you become aware of your conditioning, and try to transcend it, there are still strong psychological forces that may thwart your progress. To a large extent, your mindset is hard-wired, influenced by powerful factors outside your control such as your genes and cognitive processes.

In simple terms, we are creatures of habit. Habits are routines that we develop to help us save energy and time, so we can be more efficient. According to research at Duke University 40 per cent of our actions are governed by our habits.[13] In the words of Charles Duhigg in his book *The Power of Habit*: habits 'are so strong, in fact, that they cause our brains to cling to them at the exclusion of all else, including common sense.'[14]

Your habits are relevant to every aspect of your life and, in many ways, define your character, which means that if you want to change, you have to change your habits. And it is hard. If you have ever given up smoking or tried to stick to a weight-loss regime, you'll know how tough it is to change one simple, specific behaviour, even though you know it will be good for you.

So, how do you change, yet alone identify the hundreds of less obvious habits that drive your behaviour each day? These might include spending too much time on social media or not drinking enough water, or less obvious ones like not looking at your partner when they are talking to you or always imagining the worst scenario when faced with problems.

These responses help to get you through the day, but at the cost of limiting and automating your experience. You risk surrendering your autonomy and self-determination, as you succumb to the daily cycles of moods, worries and repetitive thoughts.

It is so easy to get trapped at your current level of consciousness, and limit your experience to a narrow focus on what is wrong with your life, and what you think needs improving. For many years, I wasted time going round and round in a circle of self-absorption, ruminating on trivial anxieties and petty concerns, while all the time oblivious to the simple wonder of being alive.

Many of us suffer from this. We fixate on the future, intent on our desires, fears and anxieties; or dwell in the past, focusing on regrets, mistakes and guilt. As you will see later, it is only by being in the present moment that you can transcend your Conditioned Self, and gain freedom from it and from the Groundhog Day Condition.

fight or flight

Over tens of thousands of years, we have learned simple rules to survive, deliberately narrowing our choices to deal with threats, so that we would not waste valuable energy analysing those choices.

The classic example of this is the fight-or-flight response: when you are faced with a challenge, your first reaction is normally to fight or to flee. This instinctive mechanism, which we share with other species, has helped us to survive over time.

We all know people who are 'fighters'. Their reality seems to reinforce the need for conflict, and they tend to be dominant, competitive and status-seeking individuals. I know many businesspeople who are only happy if they are winning, often mistaking normal everyday problems for threats to their survival, as their brains cannot distinguish between a minor dispute and life-or-death danger.

At the opposite end of the scale are those people whose natural instinct is flight. They always back down, avoiding confrontation and conflict at all cost. 'Fleers' confuse simple disagreements with threats to their survival. Their overriding need for security keeps them trapped in uncomfortable situations and relationships. Over the years, they create a reality that continually scans a seemingly hostile world for potential dangers, paralysing themselves with misplaced apprehension as they do so.

Part of your challenge in changing your behaviour is that it is frequently instinctual, determined by this evolutionary reaction. You will need to constantly override your initial fight-or-flight response if you want to make genuine progress.

held down by powerful forces

The Groundhog Day Condition is so comprehensive that it feels like the natural human condition. But is this really the case? Is this is as good as it gets? Are you destined to be a creature of habit, forever enslaved by your instincts, fears and desires?

You know what you want and you may have the knowledge and even the skills to make it happen, but still you remain stuck. Somehow, you are always being pulled back to your default state, trying to improve the quality of your experience by changing your situation. And while this will give you a temporary boost, you will soon revert to your fixed point, as the force exerted by the Groundhog Day Condition drags you back down.

Like Gulliver, you are bound by tiny ropes that you mistakenly believe are unbreakable. You are a giant in your self-made Lilliput. But it is time for you to rise above your Conditioned Self – to cut the ropes and break free of the assumptions that tie you down – and instead, think and act beyond it. Only then can you prepare the ground for genuine change.

change is hard

The reality is that diets and exercise regimes rarely work (at least not in the long term). Nor do personal and organisational change programmes have much impact for the most part. All we are doing is moving into a new space for a while, before being pulled back again to a form of homeostasis. For decades I have studied, taught and practised change management. Every time I observe participants in change programmes – whether it is going to the gym, taking up yoga or completing a leadership development course – I notice that the majority struggle to make long-term changes. Few are able to translate their intentions into action and stick with it.

In almost every case, when I interview the participants they will appear contrite, uncertain and even apologetic about why they have stopped. It is rarely due to the change programme itself, and it isn't that they don't want to improve. Sometimes they claim it is lack of time or competing demands or forgetfulness. In my view, the more probable cause is the difficulty in converting knowledge and intention into action.

Often, it can feel like there is an invisible force that prevents us from taking action, sabotaging our desires and goals. It saps our power and weakens our resolve. Stop for a moment and think about this feeling. Remember what it is like to make a resolution to get fitter. You sign up for a Pilates or spinning class and maybe go once or twice, but then you stop. When you think about going, you feel a pressure or resistance that reduces your motivation. You tell yourself you are not in the mood or you will wait until you feel better, but such a perfect time never comes.

Why do we find it so hard to become the person we want to be? We know what to do, we know how to do it and we make our plan. We are determined to press forward, yet so often abandon our plans within days or even hours. This is a common predicament and an important one. So, let's explore it in more detail.

ALIENATED FROM YOURSELF

Let's first focus on a more complex behaviour such as how you respond to assertive people. Let's say you know that you need to be more assertive. You may even have been on a course and learned a new technique. But when you are faced with a difficult colleague or your own partner, you will think about being more self-assured, but probably feel you are being pulled back to your habitual responses, which may be submissive. You may even experience the feeling of learned helplessness (see p. 33). As you learn to be more helpless, you compound the condition, and after many failed attempts to progress, you may feel like giving up and assume you can never change. You remain in your own prison under lock and key.

You may also feel alienated, like you are out of touch with yourself, others and life itself. Psychologist Erich Fromm wrote about this in the 1950s, and it is just as relevant today:

> By alienation is meant a mode of experience in which the person experiences himself as an alien. He has become, one might say, estranged from himself. He does not experience himself as the center of his world, as the creator of his own acts, but his acts and their consequences have become his masters, whom he obeys, or whom he may even worship.[15]
>
> Erich Fromm, *The Sane Society*

When you reflect on this quotation and the implications of what I am writing, you may start to wonder if you are alienated or maybe, in a sense, leading someone else's life. Are you leading the life you want, or the life you have settled for? This is challenging. Maybe your parents, your teachers, your bosses, your friends and your partner are the architects of your character, rather than you. Does it seem like you have continually adapted to other people's expectations and society's norms, and that you have lost touch with yourself? Who is really in charge? This question deserves really careful consideration.

In the words of writer and philosopher Henry David Thoreau, many people 'lead lives of quiet desperation'.[16] You may feel your own sense of quiet desperation if you are not true to yourself; you can never be free if you are leading someone else's life. This is not necessarily your fault. You may have built your own mental prison to protect yourself from your fears, but you are none the less still serving time in a gilded cage of your own making. I know, as I built a beautiful one in my thirties and stayed inside it for years.

WHO'S IN CHARGE?

Your language and self-talk reinforce your imprisonment in the Conditioned Self. You may often think and speak as though you are no longer in charge of your mind, or your life. You become disempowered when you tell yourself you 'have to' be in London for the conference next week, although you believe it to be pointless; that you 'must' accept your neighbours' invitation for dinner, even though you don't like them; and that you are 'forced' to stay in the job you loathe in order to pay off the mortgage.

There is a better way of living available to you. You can create a new story and a new vision. You just need to break free from your Conditioned Self.

the conditioned self creates its own reality

Your Conditioned Self forms its own needs and wants that can never be satisfied, such as the need to be right all the time or to be liked by everyone. Whatever you achieve, whatever you acquire, it will never be enough. This is the Groundhog Day Condition at work. It is the never-ending, repetitive and compulsive cycle of desire for more: when we have the perfect body, the perfect career, the perfect partner – then, at last, we will be happy. But it is just an illusion, and we know it. Like eating junk food, it gives us a temporary high, followed by dissatisfaction soon after. We compete in a race we can never win – a quest for the impossible dream.

Your Conditioned Self creates its own 'personal reality' – a unique system of thoughts, attitudes, emotions and values. Your personal reality filters your perception and creates your experience. It is a reflection of reality, not reality itself. So, in effect, there are two realities. The reality of 'what is' – the real world – and the world as you see it through your own eyes. For example, you might think that your colleague at work does not like you because they look angry, but, in fact, they are upset about something that happened at home and which has nothing to do with you.

As a child, you create your own reality in order to feel secure, and as a coping mechanism. As you mature into adulthood, this reality has less value, yet you may still cling to its familiar patterns. I have worked with people who never took risks and never sought a promotion because they experienced shame as children. Once hurt, they internalised the pain and spent their lives trying to avoid more shame by shunning new challenges. So the same coping mechanism that seemed to protect them as children now held them back as adults. They stayed safe to an extent, but also limited their growth and relationships.

Your personal reality determines the quality of your experience today, regulating what is good or bad, enjoyable or unpleasant. It casts its spell over all your activities and encounters, and is essential to bringing about significant personal change. Changing your Conditioned Self and its accompanying personal reality will have a far greater impact on the quality of your life than changing your circumstances.

So why not consider putting the same effort into changing your beliefs, habits and thoughts as you put into your work, your hobbies and your relationships? Imagine how great life could be if you developed a mindset that made you feel exuberant, whatever your circumstances. Imagine being the person that you look up to and would like to emulate.

five common characteristics of the conditioned self

To help you understand the nature and influence of your Conditioned Self and the personal reality it creates, I want to introduce five common characteristics that you should recognise. Phil, like most of us, displays some, but not all of them:

- Entitlement
- Approval
- Insecurity
- Dependency
- Control

I have observed one or more of these in almost everyone I have met over the years. Each is distinguished by a specific, overriding need or motivation that drives behaviour, separating us from an authentic, fulfilling life. In effect, they take charge of our minds and direct our lives in specific and generally unhelpful ways. They represent a state of consciousness that we project out onto our external reality, dictating the scope and quality of our experience and creating a huge gap in our lives, which they can never fill.

All five characteristics are our Conditioned Self's best attempt to protect our fragile self-esteem. Unfortunately, they all produce their own particular version of the Groundhog Day Condition and prevent us from achieving our full potential for a wonderful life.

ENTITLEMENT

Phil's Conditioned Self is dominated by a sense of entitlement. He is prone to selfishness, pride and a self-centredness bordering on narcissism. He believes that the more he focuses on satisfying his own needs, the happier he will become. When he arrives in town he demands the best hotel and is sarcastic to the hotel manager when she is unable to provide cappuccino or espresso.

I once knew a very wealthy lady whose self-esteem was dependent on continually getting what she wanted. Unfortunately, she never had enough. Whatever she looked like or whatever she owned, she always felt an underlying lack of self-worth. She had to be stimulated all the time, and hated to be bored or alone for even a moment. She struggled to form intimate relationships because she was too self-centred and insensitive to the needs of others. Lacking genuine connection, she sought instant gratification in activities such as shopping or partying.

The problem is that 'entitled' people place all their happiness on events outside of themselves, creating a never-ending series of expectations and needs that can never be met. Each promises fulfilment, but fails to deliver when it is achieved, leading to permanent dissatisfaction and disappointment. The key is to recognise the pattern, and catch yourself feeling a sense of entitlement. When you become more aware, you can interrupt the pattern and so let go of the need for everything to go your way. This is a much more relaxing and healthy way to live.

APPROVAL

I know many people who spend their lives overachieving, looking for the approval they never got from their parents. Desperate for attention, they become trapped in repetitive cycles of people-pleasing. Recurrent thoughts include, 'Do they like me or not?' and 'I have to be famous, wealthy, or beautiful before anyone will like me'.

A craving for approval, status and recognition can be the motivation for great success. The problem is that no amount of approval is ever enough to compensate for the lack of it in your childhood. Whatever you achieve, however beautiful you are and regardless of how much money you make, if you crave recognition you will never find peace of mind. For you have based your happiness on what others think of you, and this is always doomed to failure. Enough is never going to be enough.

This is why so many celebrities have problems. They base their self-esteem on the media's opinion of them, and a bad review or a scandal can send them into a tailspin. Whoever you are, there will always be people who disapprove of you, so don't waste your time and energy trying to change their views by being the person you *think* they want you to be.

I can endorse this because I always yearned for approval. I wanted my parents' approval, my friends' recognition and for everyone to like me. It is still a powerful drive, but one that I am far better at managing as I now accept how futile, even ridiculous, it is. Whatever I do or say, some people will like me and some won't. Like the weather, there is nothing I, or anyone else, can do about it.

INSECURITY

Many people's lives are plagued by insecurity. They suffer from recurring patterns of low self-esteem, poor self-image, loneliness and disconnection. They tend to have repetitive thoughts such as, 'I am not worthy of love', or, 'I can't make friends', or, 'I must always save money'. Their behaviour reflects their fears, as they are inclined to underachieve and are fearful of forming intimate relationships. They may even prefer to be alone, rather than risk being hurt by someone else in a new relationship.

Do you interpret the world as a hostile, fearful place? Do you feel vulnerable and yearn to run away from difficulties or responsibility? Do you want a stable, steady existence where nothing threatens the status quo? Even if this were possible, would you really choose to live this way? If this describes you, then be aware that you may be avoiding some pain, but you are avoiding spontaneity, passion and excitement as well.

DEPENDENCY

Dependent people fail to develop into fully autonomous adults. They suffer from habitual pessimism and lack confidence. They look to other people to save them, and are prone to thoughts such as, 'I need someone to look after me', or, 'If only things could be different'. They have difficulty with personal responsibility or risk, and tend to be reactive.

People with a high need for security prefer to stay in small, familiar groups, and to seek reassurance and safety. It is often hard for them to find their own answers to life's great questions, and they look instead for something or someone else to provide them. In relationships, dependent people will tend to look for the perfect partner who will 'complete them'. Even if they find such a person, the illusion rapidly disappears. If you are dependent by nature, you will find it hard to cope with the truth that your partner is imperfect, and that life is imperfect. Nobody else can provide you with the meaning and certainty you crave. You must resolve this yourself.

CONTROL

We all want and need some degree of control. (Phil wants to control the town when he becomes aware of the possibilities that the time loop gives him.) The difficulty arises if you are someone who craves too much of it.

Do you have recurring thoughts such as 'I have to be perfect in everything I do', or, 'I am only happy if I am in control?' A high need for control comes from wanting to be invulnerable, but leads to great frustration. In effect, your world and the real world are in conflict, as life rarely conforms to rigid rules of consistency, order and predictability. Seeking to control people and events to meet your needs and fit in with your personal reality is doomed to failure.

your conditioned self is in charge

In the early stages of the film Phil exemplifies the worst parts of the Conditioned Self. He is self-centred, arrogant, impatient, restless, cynical and isolated. Unknowingly, he creates his own miserable days. He expects to have a bad time and feels undervalued by the people to whom he considers himself superior. He believes Rita is an inexperienced producer and simply ignores Larry the cameraman. He avoids intimacy and connection at all costs. Like a prison cell, his Conditioned Self isolates him from others.

What is your Conditioned Self like? You will know this part of you is in charge every time you feel that you ought to act in a particular way; every time you seek other people's approval or act out of fear; every time you delay your happiness until the realisation of a goal, or play a role that is expected of you; and every time you hear that familiar inner voice judging, criticising and discouraging you.

You may tend to defend, justify and bolster your Conditioned Self, as you are convinced it is you. Its routines and recurring patterns comfort you, and form your personality through a lifetime of repetition.

You may think that you have no choice, or that you cannot break free until a distant time in the future that never comes. You have given your power away to custom and conformity, to saving face and keeping up appearances. But there is always a nagging doubt in the back of your mind that just won't go away, telling you are not living the life you want, or that you are missing out on something, making you feel detached and dissociated from what is going on around you, or like a character in a film, sticking rigidly to your roles and your lines. You are playing the part of your character as scripted in your past.

The quality of your life is dependent on the quality of your experience, and the quality of your experience is profoundly influenced by the power of your Conditioned Self. Like the Ghost in *A Christmas Carol*, you create your own chains with each decision you make. But you can also break the chains and establish new ones. Your Conditioned Self may describe your personality, but it is not your true identity or destiny.

the conditions that limit you

Your Conditioned Self puts limiting conditions on everything, especially your happiness. It demands that your outer life must be ideal for your inner life to be so: if only I got that promotion or could afford that house, then I would be happy. So a good day is when good things happen to you, and a bad day is when bad things happen. You have surrendered your sense of wellbeing to forces beyond your control. But perhaps it is time to stop trying to create the perfect conditions all the time. Such a strategy is futile, regardless of who you are or what you have.

I have found from my own experience that if I do not feel good about myself at my core, in my inner life, I will try to compensate by seeking to improve the quality of my outer life. I look to success to fix my inner problems, to alleviate my fears and boost my self-esteem. The trouble is that it never does so for more than a short while.

You cannot fix what is wrong inside of you by getting everything you *think* you want. Even if everything appeared perfect, it would be a mirage – because as soon as you think you have got there it will disappear, as new challenges, fears and anxieties inevitably arise.

You may waste a lot of your time seeking 'pseudo-satisfiers', the possessions or achievements of a consumer lifestyle that provide temporary satisfaction. You might endeavour to improve your status or gain more power. This, again, may meet your conditioned needs briefly, but does not address your authentic needs for love and meaning.[17] Only when you focus on healing your inner wounds will you find the peace of mind and joy you yearn for. When you feel good about yourself at your core, you will need nothing else.

MY STRUGGLE WITH THE CONDITION

I have struggled to feel good at my core, and have suffered from the Groundhog Day condition. I have spent many years trying to escape its tight grip, and have written this book to help myself, as well as you to do the same. It is a continuous process that never ends, but it is a journey I have never regretted taking.

I have had many extraordinary outer experiences. I built a very successful business, lived in California for five years, taught at Oxford University, home schooled my children, am a published author and enjoyed the high life in every sense of the word, yet my inner life remained stagnant for many years. I felt powerless to control my feelings, and spent more and more energy trying to rearrange my situation to give me the feelings I wanted. I became addicted to new circumstances, craving a never-ending series of distractions and experiences to fill the deep hole I felt at the centre of my being. I was looking for a saviour to lift me up into the light from the darkness that enveloped me.

As I considered my predicament, I thought again about *Groundhog Day*. The film no longer felt like just the story of Phil Connors. It felt like the story of my life. My thinking was repetitive, and in my mind I was essentially reliving the same day over and over again.

When I read the entire contents of a diary I had kept
for over ten years, I witnessed first-hand the power of
the Groundhog Day Condition. I read about all the
places I had been to – from Sydney and Singapore to
San Francisco and Santa Fe – and the hundreds of
people I had met through my work in business,
training and university.

During that time, I had lived in the UK and California,
lost my father, been divorced, made new friends and
lost contact with others, written two books, started
five businesses and shut down three. It appeared
that a great deal had happened and changed in my
life – or had it?

For I noticed something else in the diaries. In between
the record of my activities, I had written more personal
observations and, as I examined them, I realised, to my
dismay, that whereas much had changed in my outer
life, almost nothing had changed in my inner life. In
year ten, I was still writing about the same concerns as
July of year one. I still had the same hopes, fears, and
regrets. How could I be happy? How could I deal with
middle age? Why was I feeling so restless? My diary
entries followed cyclical patterns of swings between
happiness and sadness, optimism and pessimism,
action and withdrawal. In my inner life, I was trapped
in my own version of Phil Connors's repetitive day.

My diary enabled me to see that underneath the superficial variety of my life, there was an inescapable sameness, irrespective of where I was or what I was doing. (I recommend you keep a diary or a journal too, to help you discern patterns in your life that would otherwise remain hidden as you are too busy to notice them.)

Being in Hawaii did not break me free, nor did seeing my first book in print. Each morning I would wake up with the same feeling that I had little or no control over my moods or actions. I would get up to shower, eat breakfast and then sit down at the computer. The rest of the day would follow the same routine of answering emails, surfing the net, doing admin and taking the odd break. Then it was evening, and another day had disappeared. It felt as though I was living life unconsciously and missing the whole point of it.

The truth was that I had spent my life creating what I believed were the ideal circumstances for contentment, only to discover that they were an illusion. They had little or no bearing on my happiness. I had reached the finishing line, but I had been running in the wrong race.

It has taken me many years to recognise the deeper patterns of the Condition and to realise that I was caught in short-term repetitions such as addiction to new ideas and a compulsion to respond to emails immediately. I was also trapped in much deeper, longer-term patterns (such as the constant search for a new project, a new diversion to make me happy) and obsessed by an endless search for novelty and new experiences. It was my way of easing the pain.

For many years, I would start a new job or create a new business as a way of fixing my life. For the first few weeks or months everything was exciting, and the buzz gave me a huge rush of adrenaline. By constantly moving, I could avoid dealing with the deeper patterns. But inevitably, this led to tremendous stress, then illness, and I would crash soon after, taking a few weeks to recover. All would be calm and balanced for a while, and then I would be off again on another pursuit for the big answer to my existence.

The problem was that I had attained all my goals. Through hard work and luck, I had accomplished everything I had set out to achieve and much more. I was healthy, wealthy, married and a father. But I was no happier. I still felt empty and alienated, yearning for more and more successes that I hoped would make me happy.

Over the last five years I have largely broken free and so I write from direct, personal experience. My old personal reality was of no use any more. It had failed me. I reached a point so low that I had to change. There was no alternative. My fortunes reversed significantly and I lost a great deal. Yet the unravelling of my old outer life paved the way for a far richer, more rewarding inner life.

Countless studies demonstrate, again and again, that wealth, status and achievement do not lead to happiness and fulfilment. What made things worse was that I knew this all along. I was teaching and writing about these lessons of positive psychology, yet was still looking to the symbols of success to make me feel better.

For me, *Groundhog Day* also represents resisting the repetitive pressures of our materialist culture. It is the feeling that I have no choice but to achieve more, consume more and prove my worth.

Until you translate knowledge into new habits and behaviour – you will stay caught in your own Groundhog Day. Happiness will be something you read about, and are even an expert on, but you will not feel it. Like watching cookery shows on TV, but never going in the kitchen, you will remain an observer of your life, not a participant in it.

My hope for you is not that you acquire more know-ledge. No, my hope is that you experience genuine joy, peace of mind and wellbeing and that you make the changes in your life that will give you sustainable happiness.

the prognosis

If you don't change your beliefs, your life will be like this forever. Is that good news?[18]
W. Somerset Maugham, novelist and playwright

How do you think your life will turn out if you continue on your current course? You may be entirely happy and not want to make any changes. That's wonderful, but maybe there is something nagging away in the back of your mind. I know that I have not always been honest with myself.

Yet there is a part of you and I, deep within our core, that is just delighted to be alive and that needs nothing more. This is the part of you that blossomed before all your conditioning and habits took hold of you. This is your Authentic Self and it still has a voice, however subdued.

Today you have a choice. Do you stay on your present course or do you change direction? What do you really want? How about moving beyond your Conditioned Self and finding your voice. Go beyond the details and content of your days. Go beyond the expectations, obligations and duties that tie you down. What is your voice telling you? Maybe it is whispering to you: 'This is not right. Remember who you are. You need to wake up.'

Until you address the root causes of the Groundhog Day Condition, you will continue to live the same day in your head. Whatever is happening around you, you cannot escape from the daily cycles of conditioning, personality, moods, feelings and thoughts. My question to you is this: do you want to have a year of genuine progress and fully engaged experience? Or do you want a year of the same day's experience repeated three hundred and sixty-five times?

Phil's inner Groundhog Day Condition prevents him from escaping his outer time trap. He has to break away from the former to free himself from the latter, and I have had to do the same. I reached the conclusion that I would never be truly happy or fulfilled if I remained captive in a prison of my own making.

So, it is up to you. If you do not deal with the Condition, you will continue to experience the same thoughts, feelings and behaviours as you do today. When circumstances are going your way, you will be happy; when they are not, you won't be. After many years of struggle, I now know that this is not how you find fulfilment.

breaking free

The rest of this book is focused on how you too can break free from your conditioning, and fully engage with life. There is no quick fix here. If you want to liberate yourself from your own Groundhog Day, you need to transform how you live your life, and this means transforming how you think, feel and act every day, as Phil did.

You can decide what matters most, and how you want to live from this day on. When you let your Authentic Self flourish, you can overcome any limits that have held you back and unlock your full potential for happiness and fulfilment.

accepting you have the condition

If you are ready, the first step is to be honest yourself. Do you know the real reasons why you are not satisfied with your life? As I've said, I have had to deal with divorce, business failures and serious personal problems, and I know how difficult it can be when you face facts. In each case, my first reaction was denial or to blame circumstances. It was only when I took responsibility for what had gone wrong and stopped blaming other people, or the economy, that I could create a solid base for moving forward. Living in denial is building a future on self-deception. You can only make lasting changes when you are honest with yourself and move beyond your defensive patterns.

You also have to be clear about what you can and can't change. In my own case, as this became clearer, I found that much of what I had taken for granted started to unravel in front of me. I began to question my lifestyle, my work, my dreams, my relationships, my decisions and every important aspect of my life. I kept on having the nagging thought, 'This is not me. This is not the life I want.' This is subversive, but also liberating.

Groundhog Day is a series of wake-up calls, continuing crises and challenges for Phil. Eventually, he realises that he has not treated the Condition itself, but has been lost in its pathology, and that pushes him in a direction that ultimately leads to his transformation. What is going to do the same for you? When are you going to reach that point when you have no choice other than transformation?

choose freedom

There are many different changes you may want in your life, yet the biggest benefit of treating the Groundhog Day Condition is gaining freedom: the freedom to choose your thoughts, your actions and be yourself, and the freedom to live your authentic life and to be fulfilled and unconditionally happy.

This can be daunting, as it means taking responsibility for your decisions and your actions (or inaction), and for the life you make for yourself. Freedom requires that you transcend your circumstances, conditioning and habits. You then have the opportunity to engage with life.

This freedom is your birthright. Your Authentic Self is already free. You just need to reconnect to it. Freedom also means removing the conditions that keep you tied down. You are so much more than your conditioning: you are not your thoughts, your beliefs, your habits and your behaviours; neither are you your job title, your personal role or your daily routine. You are far greater than the sum of your parts.

You will feel free when you acknowledge that your Conditioned Self can never create a perfect life. And only you can do this by thinking and feeling differently about the life you are living now.

choose unconditional happiness

> Each morning when I open my eyes I say to myself: I, not events, have the power to make me happy or unhappy today.[19]
>
> Groucho Marx, comedian and film star

When you have decided you want freedom, your next question may well be: 'Freedom to do what?'

Let me suggest an answer. You are now free to be happy. So why not choose to be unconditionally happy? This does not mean you will be happy all the time. What it does mean is that you take responsibility for your own happiness by no longer making it dependent on your circumstances, conditioning or old habits. When you disengage from your Conditioned Self, you also disengage from conditional happiness. Like Phil, you can create your own world of peace, calm, wellbeing and joy whatever is happening around you. Your sense of wellbeing no longer needs to rely on a series of rules and conditions you have imposed and which are impossible to meet on a consistent basis.

My problem was that I wanted to be happy, but I felt like I was lost in a desert without a compass, wandering aimlessly in this direction or that. My conditioning had administered a seductive anaesthetic that kept me unconscious, consumed by a hopeless search for an oasis that was a mirage all the time. The mirage had been created by my Conditioned Self's definition of happiness, which was a doomed yearning for constant pleasure and comfort. My insatiable need for security, status and control trumped every other need, especially my declared desire to be happy.

I had to make the choice to be unconditionally happy. It's not easy, but it is the only way, and if you are committed to being happy, you will have to do the same. Make this your highest priority. Choose happiness over wealth, power, status, approval, control and security. Only when you renounce any and all conditions, can you – by definition – be unconditionally happy.

You also need to make a firm commitment. When Phil commits to his own happiness, his world is transformed. You too can do this. Ask yourself these simple questions every day:

- Do I want to be rich or do I want to be happy?
- Do I want a high quality of life or a high quality of experience?

You can choose between these two paths every day and the choices you make will lead you in markedly different directions. This is critical as you need to make the right choice repeatedly to break the old patterns and establish new ones that support your commitment.

If you are not sure about this choice, ask yourself some simple questions that you must answer yes or no to as follows ('wealthy' means being, say, in the top 1 per cent income bracket in your country; 'average' means a median income):

- Would I rather be wealthy and unhealthy, or average and healthy?
- Would I rather be wealthy and depressed, or average and contented?

- Would I rather be wealthy and unhappily married, or average and happily married?
- Would I rather be wealthy in a career I loathe, or earn an average salary in a career I love?
- Would I rather be wealthy and feel stressed, overworked and out of balance, or average, feeling calm and balanced?

In essence, when you are asked to explicitly opt for wealth over health, wellbeing, relationships, career and quality of life it seems obvious that money is less important. The problem is that you soon forget this and drift back to spending your time, energy and focus on making money, at the expense of the positive feelings outlined above. This is your Conditioned Self at work again, like gravity pulling you back to your default mode.

If you look outside of yourself for your happiness, you will only find short-term, temporary pleasure. If you look within, searching for happiness without conditions, you will discover long-term joy and even bliss. Forget about just coping or getting through. You were born with the resources to flourish.

Unconditional happiness is the natural outcome of living authentically. This is what distinguishes a 'happy life' from a feeling of happiness. Phil feels good by doing good. He focuses less on *being* happy, and more on living a good life. I recommend you do the same.

make it urgent

One of my favourite maxims is, 'Life is not a dress rehearsal'. If you are serious about changing, you also need to create some urgency. In the fictional world of Punxsutawney, Phil can prepare for each day like a play with the same actors, scripts and drama. For you and I, there are no rehearsals, and appreciating what this means is imperative.

As the song says, 'Enjoy yourself. It's later than you think'.[20] You may associate enjoyment with travel, partying or a fancy new home. Whatever enjoyment means to you, you should stop to reflect on the life you want to lead.

What advice would you give to a close friend if they were living your exact life? What advice would you give yourself if you knew you had only a few months to live? My advice is that if you want to be happier, then improve the quality of your moment-to-moment experience by letting go of your Conditioned Self. Unconditional happiness will sustain you throughout good and bad times, and is the secret to successful ageing.

You have the power to enhance the quality of your life. Whatever hardship you are facing today, do not give up. There is always hope, however dire you think things are. And you always have a choice.

Even when trapped in time for eternity, Phil maintains hope and finds a better way of living. He eventually accepts that he cannot control his circumstances, so is forced to make the best of them. In doing so, he not only learns to survive, he moves to a higher level of consciousness that is also available to you and me.

It does not matter where or how you are today, you can do the same. So it's time to move beyond your own self-imposed conditions and escape. It's time to disengage from the Groundhog Day Condition and engage with your Authentic Self and the incredible world all around you. Because whether you are ill, broke, depressed or at the end of your tether, life *can* be better for you. This is the promise of the film and the promise of my book.

SUMMARY

- There are three main causes of the Groundhog Day Condition:

  - Your circumstances (such as your career, finances and relationships)
  - Your conditioning (such as your parenting and education)
  - Your mind (your cognitive processes and preference for habituation)

- If you do not address the Condition you will continue to experience the same quality of thoughts and feelings for the rest of your life.

- Change is hard and you are held down by forces exerted by your Conditioned Self.

- There are five common characteristics of the Conditioned Self:

  - ◆ Entitlement
  - ◆ Approval
  - ◆ Security
  - ◆ Dependency
  - ◆ Control

- Be clear about what you really want. Let go of any need to impress, and for power or control or approval. What do *you* want?

- If you want to transcend the Groundhog Day Condition, you need to accept that you are stuck and then commit to unconditional happiness above all else.

CHAPTER FOUR

quality time

We shall not cease from exploration, and the end of
all our exploring will be to arrive where we started
and know the place for the first time.

T. S. Eliot, playwright and poet

All my life I have been an explorer. I have been searching for
the perfect life, constantly moving to new places, starting
new careers and seeking new lifestyles. It has taken me over
fifty years to know my place for the first time, and to discover
that the perfect life was always available, right in front of
me. Now I know that I already have everything in order to
be happy and fulfilled. I do not need any more money, power,
status or approval. All I required was a set of directions, and
I found them in *Groundhog Day*.

My exploration has brought me back to the here and now.
Instead of always planning my future, I am engaging with
the present moment, slowing down and appreciating what I
have. This is the first stage of leading a fully engaged life

– I had to learn how to engage with the moment-to-moment unfolding of my life before I could engage with myself and with others effectively. When you engage with life, you can do so much more with what you already have, and make the best of the life you are leading now. Above all, you can experience your life in new ways that increase your ability to be happier without changing anything other than your perspective.

Groundhog Day highlights the contrast between two ways of living: being disengaged and being engaged. You always have this choice before you. At any point today, you can switch from being disengaged to being engaged. For most of his time in Punxsutawney Phil is disengaged. He is disconnected from the town and its people. Over the course of the film, he starts to connect to what was happening around him and to other people. He becomes more passionate, spontaneous and loving as he learns to live life to the full. Of course, he had this capacity all along, but simply had to let go of his old Conditioned Self.

You can transform your life too. All the clues and all the resources you need are in the film if you look closely. Phil, as we know, repeats the same day thousands of times and learns, eventually, that he can improve the quality of each moment without altering his circumstances. He learns to make the best use of the time he has. I call this 'quality time'.

When you quieten your mind and stop living in the past or

future, becoming fully present in the now, you create your own quality time. Then you can find it easier to make the space for genuine change and engage with life, enabling you to appreciate what you already have, rather than fixating on what you don't have. Phil discovers joy in the commonplace details of his everyday life, and so can you. All you have to do is wake up to the wonder and beauty all around you.

I have done my best to remove the restrictions and rules that my Conditioned Self has imposed. In this chapter, I will help you to do the same. You will learn how to be more appreciative of what you have already, and less anxious to have more, achieve more or be more. Whatever you are doing, wherever you are and whoever you are with, you can learn how to make each moment of your life better and be happier.

accepting your reality

Groundhog Day makes visible the pain and suffering that Phil had previously tried, and failed, to conceal through distraction. He spends years resisting his reality. At different times, he is angry, in denial, bitter and confrontational. He tries every manipulation and trick until he realises that he can't change or control reality. Having fought reality, he learns to accept it and then to love it as he engages with 'what is' not 'what ought to be'.

Phil accepts that pain is not just a part of life, but that it can also be the catalyst for fundamental change. Adversity

77

provides the opportunity to heal and grow. Only through accepting reality and taking on the great challenges he faces can he progress.

So, a first step to letting go of your old Conditioned Self is simply to allow yourself to fully acknowledge your emotions, no matter how painful they are. Often, when you sense a powerful emotion, such as fear or anger, you want to challenge or repress it. Some people avoid painful emotions through addictions like drink, drugs, shopping or sex; I used to escape into projects like starting a business or a house renovation. However, this only serves to give the emotion more power. A healthier response is to be in tune with your emotions, not run away from them. Try giving yourself all the time you need to experience and accept your feelings. It is the holding back of feelings that is limiting, and the release that is liberating.

We need to be honest with ourselves and we also need to stop resisting reality, and to embrace it instead. Phil cannot escape or be in denial. However he tries to distract himself, whether through gluttony, promiscuity or other diversions, he can't escape the time loop. Once the distractions no longer amuse him, he has no choice but to confront the true extent of his predicament and face his fears head-on.

If you want to change your life, you will need to face yours too. By accepting reality and acknowledging that your Conditioned Self is failing you, you take personal responsibility for changing yourself. This is a defining moment.

You can jump-start the process of personal change when you recognise that you see the world through your own personal reality as presented by your Conditioned Self. By selecting what you want to see, hear and feel (as we all do) you distort reality, using your biases, values and other preferences to make sense of your world.

PERSONAL REALITY AT WORK

I remember watching *Groundhog Day* with a friend who saw it as a mildly amusing Bill Murray comedy: what I found extraordinary, especially the repetition, he found uninteresting; when I laughed out loud, my friend was silent. We were both watching the same film, but through the different filters of our own personal realities. We had different expectations and standards for evaluating the film and, consequently, different interpretations and opinions of it. Extend this phenomenon from a film that only lasts 101 minutes to a lifetime of accumulated experiences, and you can begin to appreciate the significance of your personal reality.

Of course, your Conditioned Self is not all bad. Your conditioning gave you language, an education and the practical knowledge to function and survive. The problem lies more in the unintended consequences, such as how your conditioning limits your awareness. In order to conform to social and cultural norms, you can unwittingly restrict your awareness and disengage from what could be a far richer life. Some people call this your comfort zone. I call it the Groundhog Day Condition.

full-spectrum living

Repetitive patterns of habitual thinking can project a mind-numbing reality when, instinctively, you know that there is a far greater potential for fulfilment, and it sometimes feels that it is just beyond your reach. I call this greater potential 'full-spectrum living' and it means experiencing all that life has to offer, even the tough parts like sadness and disappointment.

When you are stuck in autopilot mode, rushing around from one activity to another, you cannot enjoy full-spectrum living. When you slow down, and are present, you can start to pay more attention to what is really before you in the here and now, and less to your personal reality. For you are not just your habits, beliefs or thoughts. You are free to face life head-on – free to be open to the unlimited possibilities before you. And I believe that exploring these possibilities and being fully engaged is the purpose of our lives, the natural goal for all of us. Psychologist Abraham Maslow called this self-actualisation:

> All the evidence that we have indicates that it is
> reasonable to assume in practically every human
> being, and certainly in almost every newborn baby,
> that there is an active will toward health, an impulse
> towards growth, or toward . . . actualization.[21]

it's about time

At its heart, the wisdom of *Groundhog Day* encourages you to change how you experience time which, in turn, improves the quality of your experience of life. Time is the organising principle of our lives, and it also seems to move at different speeds. When you are bored it is slow. When you are excited it goes much faster. (How time flies!) If you have little moment-to-moment awareness, time seems to pass you by altogether.

Many people take each day for granted. I know I have. Days quietly slip by, turning into weeks, months and years, while you are 'living in your head'. You go to sleep each night and wake up each morning preoccupied with thoughts, largely unaware of the day ahead, other than as a series of activities or tasks to move you forward to tomorrow.

We live in a world rigidly structured by time, where so much of what we do is geared towards outcomes in the future. Think about it for a moment. How much of your time do you spend working and living for the future? Do you work to buy a bigger house, a better car, to pay for your children's education, to finance your retirement?

Time has a very strong influence over who we are and how we define ourselves: we are a complex interplay of the past (who we have been until now), the present (who we are in each moment) and the future (who we have the potential to be). We shift between each of these in subtle ways, and we all have a preferred mode that likes to take charge.

This preferred mode will also influence how we value our time. If we are future-oriented, we may see today as just another twenty-four hours as we move towards a vision of how we imagine life could be. If, however, we prefer the present mode, we may see today as a priceless gift to be cherished. We may not need a vision to motivate us, as we are content with how our lives are now.

Each stage in Phil's transformation involves an invaluable lesson about time. At first, it is an irritation to be endured, as he waits impatiently to return to his former life as a celebrity weatherman in the city. Then time is a resource, which he can use to exploit others. Next, it is a terrible burden to be suffered for eternity. Finally, time is a great gift, which he can use to learn new skills like ice sculpting, to help others and, ultimately, to find happiness.

As he becomes aware that time is a gift, he learns to master it. He slows down and pays attention to the present. He reframes his attitude completely, so what was previously a terrible day becomes a really great one. Finally, he discovers how to use his time wisely so he is able to lead a fulfilling life in each moment.

By the end of the film, Phil has stopped looking to the future. He is not concerned about how life might be, because that choice has been taken from him. And he no longer believes that he will only be happy when he has left town, or when he has won the big job promotion. Indeed, it is only when his future is removed that he can recognise the gift of the present. What had appeared dreadful is now marvellous, and he tells Rita, 'No matter what happens tomorrow, or for the rest of my life, I'm happy now because I love you.'

This is a pivotal stage in the film. Phil is happy with the present moment, with life as it is, not as it might be or should be. He has become conscious by living in the moment and paying attention. His senses are open and he savours each minute.

Do you regard time as something to be overcome, or to be endured? Do you lose yourself in a frantic race against time, as you attempt in vain to get everything done within a set period? Maybe you see each hour, each day and each week as the building blocks to construct your imagined perfect life at some time in the future, instead of regarding your time as a series of present moments to be experienced and savoured? Ask yourself this: do you want to control time or embrace it? Is the present moment a means to an end or an end in itself?

I'm going to help you learn to do what Phil did – to transform your perception of time, so that you can enhance your moment-to-moment experience and enjoy more 'quality time' for the rest of your life.

no time like the present

Mastering time starts with an acknowledgment that there is no time like the present. The *Groundhog Day* time loop is a metaphor for the present moment. Punxsutawney is the eternal now.

Phil lives in the everlasting presence of the same repeating day, and once he has adjusted to his reality he flourishes. Confined in time, Phil has no choice but to engage with the present moment. He has a past, but it becomes increasingly less relevant as he repeats the same day over and over again. Similarly, his future is of little significance, since there are no consequences to his actions beyond the twenty-four hours he inhabits. This one day *is* his life. There is no tomorrow.

Living for ever on repeat helps Phil to discover that there is no better time to be happy than right now, that there is no finer moment than this one and that the only path to sustainable happiness lies in the present.

This is not easy to grasp when you have got used to a way of life that separates you from the now. How much of your time is spent thinking about the past or the future as a distraction to avoid the present? When you are on your own, is your first impulse to look at your phone, turn on the TV, listen to music, go on Facebook – anything to distract yourself?

What exists beyond distractions? What is there for you outside the activities you fill your days with? The answer is found in the difference between doing and being. When you are preoccupied with doing, you lose sight of the small, ever-present moments that are available to enjoy now. When you are preoccupied with being, on the other hand, you are absorbed in the enjoyment of now. No longer are you comparing the present to a desired future or a happier past. Instead, you shift your focus to the immediate quality of your experience. When you move from doing to being, you engage with life directly and discover, like Phil, that there is no better time than now.

I have learned that the way I think about time has a significant impact on the quality of my life. Previously, I structured my time in a way that prevented me from paying attention to the present moment. It was all too easy to focus on the future, looking at life in terms of years or decades, planning for a desired future in that time to come.

Do you focus on the contrasts between where you are today and where you were before, or where you want to be? If so, you will find it hard to be present. Alternatively, maybe your focus is on events over the next year, like planned holidays, work schedules or school calendars, prioritising specific upcoming events, while regarding current moments as a means to an end – that end being your desired future? Perhaps you organise your life so you can be productive, perceiving time as a resource to be used efficiently? If so, then again, you are missing out on the present and the full spectrum of your life.

Even more concerning is the feeling you are just getting through life, day to day – living for the weekend, perhaps, regarding weekdays as a drudge until it's Friday evening, when you can 'be yourself'? Whatever your perspective, your appreciation of time will be restricted by your Conditioned Self.

You can also create your own time trap by freezing your self-image and your world view in episodes from your past. Childhood experiences often lead to rigid attitudes and even anxiety. For example, I remember being bullied in my teens because I had terrible acne. Not only was my face scarred for many years, but so was my self-image. Consequently, I wore a beard until my early forties, and even though the pockmarks are barely visible I still feel self-conscious today, to the extent that whenever I look in the mirror as a fifty-five-year-old, it can still seem like my thirteen-year-old self is looking back at me. I feel frozen in time.

So, it is only when you are in the present moment that you can wake up and come alive. Your freedom is firmly rooted in the present where you have the potential to be who you want to be today. When you see your life as a series of present moments, each one being significant, then you can engage with life as it is. This does not mean that you stop planning ahead or organising your time. You just need to restore the balance back to the present, as ultimately that is all you have.

the present moment sets you free

The greatest hindrance to living is expectancy, which depends upon the morrow and wastes today.[22]

Seneca, Roman philosopher

If you live in the present moment, you are free. In the present moment, there are no problems, no worries, just the experience of being alive and the direct experience of time. You awaken to the childlike joy of being spontaneous, curious and enthusiastic. Quite simply, you come alive again. This is your Authentic Self.

You are also more creative. When you are in the moment you are enjoying what psychologists call the state of 'flow.'[23] You are completely absorbed, losing track of time and self-consciousness. In the flow you are centred on the doing of a task, rather than its outcome. As such, you are engrossed in the act of living itself, rather than worrying about your own needs and concerns. Like Phil, who is in the flow on his last 2 February in Punxsutawney, you lose your sense of self and time and are fully in the now.

your moment-to-moment choice

As you become more present-minded, you may begin to recognise that you have a critical choice every day, every hour and every minute: the choice to focus your attention and energy on your outer world or on your inner experience.

Phil shifts his focus to the quality of his inner experience, rather than his circumstances, and you can try the same yourself. Let's take a look at how this works in practice.

Imagine today is your last day of work before flying to Majorca tomorrow for a holiday. Each moment of this day, you oscillate between eager anticipation and impatience to get home. You feel little presence or appreciation. You are delaying such feelings until your holiday begins. Everything is on hold until a projected moment in the near future – this may be when you leave work, or when you have packed your bags, or you are in the taxi going to the airport; it may be when you have got through security, and are sitting on the plane with a glass of wine; or perhaps you are delaying your pleasure until you have arrived in Majorca, or are in your hotel room or lying on the beach.

What will be the moment when you allow yourself to be appreciative? Let's assume it will be when you are on the beach. Then, let's call your current moment in the office Moment O and your moment on the beach Moment B. Now, which is better: Moment O or Moment B? Of course, you will say Moment B is better.

But is it? Maybe it is the contrast effect at work here: you feel happy in being on a beach in sunny Majorca in contrast to doing paperwork in your office on a grey, rainy day.[24] But following on from this, how would you compare Moment O in your office to being in a hospital bed with a critical illness? Then you would say Moment O is better, but only in contrast to what you perceive to be a miserable experience. The moment is the same, but the contrast makes it appear different.

All the time we are comparing moments. So, instead of comparing Moment O to B, why not compare it to one in the past when you were unemployed, ill or suffering misfor-tune? You may find that this improves the quality of Moment O, in the same way that you diminished it when you compared it to Moment B.

Now, let's go further. Why not try accepting Moment O, and every moment, as it is, suspending all judgment. This is one of the key ideas underpinning the concept of mindfulness. Jon Kabat Zinn, a leading exponent of the practice, explains: 'Mindfulness means paying attention in a particular way; on purpose, in the present moment, and non-judgmentally.'[25] As soon as we form a judgment about time, we are comparing one moment to another, but when we are mindful, we treat them all the same, becoming aware of the gift of every moment, and enjoying each one so much more.

Let's look at Moment O again. You are in the office doing boring paperwork. You loathe it, but it has got to be done. Your mind wanders to Moment B when you will be on holiday. You then interpret Moment O negatively, generating a range of feelings including resentment, frustration, regret and, most notably, the desire to be somewhere else.

This is a moment of truth, and your life is a series of such moments. You can place your attention and your energy into wishing things were different. You can distract yourself or procrastinate. You can delay satisfaction until Moment B arrives. But the problem is that aside from wasting your life away, you can never be sure that Moment B will deliver the feelings you want. What if the beach is crowded? What if it is raining? What if you take your stress with you on holiday? And even if conditions are ideal and the moment *is* perfect, will you appreciate it? Or will you be thinking about the next Moment B in the hotel restaurant, or on tomorrow's boat trip? Will the perfect moment evaporate as soon as it arrives?

You may have spent thousands of pounds on potentially happy moments in Majorca when, for no cost at all, you can boost the quality of your non-holiday moments. You may travel the world and visit every country, but the more exhilarating and transformative journey is the journey within.

So maybe it is time to try something different. If you must interpret Moment O, for example, why not appreciate that you have a job and that you can afford to go on holiday, or consider the paperwork as only one aspect of your job, and that completing it is moving you forward in your career.

Or, better still, just be present and complete the task without any interpretation at all. Consider learning how to be more mindful. It took me until my early fifties to start practising mindfulness. I have a very long way to go, but I can confirm already that this wonderful practice is more valuable than any exotic holiday. If you develop this simple skill (see p. 94), you can start to make every moment a holiday moment, making time work *for* you, not against you.

Groundhog Day is the story of turning the worst O moment into the best B moment. And a good day is measured not by the quantity of B moments, but by the quality of every moment.

quality of experience

Traditional definitions of quality of life depend on achieving your outcomes and reaching your destination. In contrast, quality of experience places the emphasis on your journey through life itself – because it is the experience that counts, not the event or the result.

Phil does not improve his standard of living; he doesn't acquire more possessions or achieve more status. No, his circumstances remain the same, yet he vastly improves the quality of his experience. And you can too.

When you are present, you are more aware and this creates quality time. This is the source of genuine happiness. A particularly profound insight of the film is that you can be happy whatever your situation. Despite his predicament, Phil is still able to be happy. He just has to learn how. He does not wait for fortune to turn in his favour. He chooses to make the best of his misfortune, and realises that he is far more fortunate than he ever imagined. He *chooses* to be happy and it all starts with his discovery of quality time.

Phil enjoys quality time when he begins to appreciate the precious value of each second of his life. He stops thinking of the past he has lost and the future he will never have. He thinks of this one day, this one hour, this one second, and cherishes them all. It does not matter whether he is doing exactly the same as he did yesterday, or as he will be doing tomorrow. Time might have stood still, but he is not going to put his life on hold too. He liberates himself from the shackles of time and no longer needs to reference the past or the future to make sense of what he is doing. Time is a continuous series of moments he can enjoy for their own value. And he is happy now.

You may have thought of quality time as time spent with your family, or being on holiday or pursuing a favourite pastime, and yes, it is all of those things, but why wait for conditions to be exactly right? Quality time is not determined by the people you are with, the job you hold or the place where you live. Instead, it depends on how you feel at any given point in each day. You cannot easily change your conditioning, as it is the sum of all the complex influences that have shaped you up till now, and it can be hard to change your circumstances – but you can change your inner experience and increase your quality time.

Why not regard this second, right now, with the same affection as you would if you were running barefoot on a tropical beach or making love on your honeymoon? Quality time is making the most of each second. It is understanding that each one offers you the choice to be aware or unaware, to be accepting or wanting and, above all, to be appreciative or unappreciative.

Why discriminate between quality and non-quality time? Why set any conditions? Why not focus instead on improving the quality of *all* your time, and making every moment count. How much time is lost in longing for other moments or feeling you ought to be doing something else? Be in the right place at the right time. The place is here and the time is now!

mindfulness in practice

You can only fully engage with life when you are awake in the present moment. It is the one refuge you have from incessant thinking, worrying and desiring. These are cravings that can never be satisfied, and they lead to permanent dissatisfaction. If your thoughts are compulsive, you may suffer from what psychologists call 'rumination' that can be damaging to your sense of wellbeing.[26] So, if you want to find peace of mind, there is always a sanctuary for you. It is the now and you can get there by practising mindfulness.

When I practise mindfulness I gain freedom from the tyranny of incessant thinking and relentless activity. For, it is only when I stop thinking, even if just for a few seconds, that I can enjoy peace of mind. I do whatever I can to ensure nothing or nobody disturbs my peace of mind. Creating moments of peace, brief 'time out' each day, engages me with the present moment, and I recommend that you do the same. Let's try a quick exercise:

Focus on your breathing, counting to five as you breathe, holding your breath for five, and five again as you breathe out. For ten seconds shut your eyes, as you breathe in and out. Do it now. Notice any thoughts and let them go by shifting your attention from a thought to a feeling in your body. Just sense the tips of your fingers, or notice your breath going in or out.

Next, do it again but this time for thirty seconds. When you have finished, do the exercise for a minute. Then two minutes.

Notice how you feel when you do this exercise, and notice that you can change your state of mind, your mood and your experience of time. You can engage with your life when you step out of the stream of relentless thinking and busyness. You don't need to be at a spa or on a meditation retreat. You can engage with your sense of aliveness any place and any time.

Mindfulness is one of your ultimate natural resources waiting to be discovered. It is your innate ability to deliberately switch from thinking to being.

My favourite practice is mindful walking. I enjoy the same walk every day and I engage with every detail of my world. I look at the clouds, feel the wind, listen to the birdsong and notice each footstep. Phil also engages with his world by walking around the town. With each step, he becomes immersed in the intimate details of everyday life. He begins to see what he previously missed, and learns to love the town he previously despised.

Have you ever disliked a place at first and then grown to like and even love it through familiarity? Wherever you live, I recommend that you get to know that place through walking its streets and paths.

two walks

At first, Phil is walking just to get to work, so he can report the Groundhog Day ceremony. He is buried in thought, oblivious to the place and the people. By the end of the film, he is walking mindfully and is fully immersed in his surroundings. I suggest that you try both types of walking too.

Let's look at the differences between taking a thirty-minute walk in doing mode and in being mode. Just like *Groundhog Day*, the walk is exactly the same: the location, distance, time and weather conditions are identical. The only difference is you.

• **Doing mode**: when you take the walk in doing mode, your mind is elsewhere, preoccupied with work or personal issues. You take your phone with you in case anyone tries to contact you, and you regularly look at your watch to make sure you get back in time. When you start, you notice that it is sunny and that reminds you that you need to book your holiday in Greece. Then you think about how much sunnier it is in Greece and how it would be warmer there. Maybe you need to move to Greece or at least buy a holiday home. But you can't afford it. And you start thinking about why you can't afford it. You didn't get the raise you were expecting and you are angry as you had worked so hard. Maybe you need to look for a new job so you can afford to get a holiday home. Then you check your phone for texts and emails and notice that you have an email from your boss. You stop to read it and discover that they want you to attend a meeting on Monday.

You start thinking about this meeting and what it could be about. What have you done wrong? Are you going to be fired? You ruminate on this for about ten minutes until you have convinced yourself that you have to get a new job. You arrive back home lost in thought. It is still sunny, but your mood is anything but!

• **Being mode**: you notice that it is sunny and you feel the rays on your skin, and observe the sunlight reflected in the stream and the plants around you. You are grateful for the warmth and for the slight breeze that comes and goes. You are aware of the sound of birds in the distance and also some children laughing. Then the sun disappears for a few seconds and you look at the clouds slowly drifting across the sky. The sun reappears and everything changes around you. It is even more beautiful when it comes back again from behind the cloud. The clouds are very high up and you then spot a plane and a very faint rumbling noise. As you turn back home you feel a sense of peace and calm that is wonderful and, as you pay attention to each step you take, you experience the joy of coming home.

You are engaging with life, and with a mode of being that is always there for you. You are returning to the present moment and to your senses. And it feels great.

I know these two walks well. Everything is the same except for the level of awareness. When you switch from doing mode to being mode, you expand your awareness. So do whatever you can to spend more of your time in being mode and less in doing mode. You can achieve this state by walking, yoga or formal meditation. You can also get there by looking at clouds rolling by or listening to birdsong. Simply pay full attention to the sounds, sights and feelings of your direct experience. Take your attention away from thinking about the type of bird that is singing, and just listen intently to its song. It takes practice, and you will find it hard, as you will slip back to doing mode all the time. That's normal. Just keep on returning to simply being and it will get a lot easier. You can try this while you are walking, swimming, at the gym or wherever is best for you.

Over time, you will notice that you can maintain your composure and peace of mind whatever is happening around you. Your boss may be shouting, a customer complaining or a driver cutting you up. It won't affect you as you will be completely present and calm. Living your life with this balance will restore your spirits and your wellbeing more than any holiday or luxury spa could ever do. Your outer life may change little each day, but it won't matter so much as you will be able to transform your inner experience and feel your best every day.

the mindful way

Compared to what we ought to be, we are half awake.[27]
William James,
American philosopher and psychologist

When you are mindful, you can see that everything is fleeting. Your fears, worries, desires and regrets come and go, and you realise that they are not you. As you pay deliberate attention to them and avoid judgment or interpretation, you shine a bright light that melts them away like snow in the warmth of the sun. Understanding and awareness bring you peace of mind.

Mindfulness is the antidote to the constrictive nature of the Groundhog Day Condition that pressures you to focus on the past and the future. It broadens your experience by helping you stay grounded in the present. When you are mindful, you are able to consciously choose where to place your attention. You can disrupt negative patterns of thinking and emotions, and replace them with more positive ones. Being mindful gives you the space to grow, to escape your conditioning and gain true freedom.

THE MINDFUL WAY TO WELLBEING

Extensive studies demonstrate that mindfulness promotes physical and mental wellbeing. When you

---

focus on your breath, your body and the sounds and sights around you, you feel content and calm. Practising mindfulness lowers stress and blood pressure, reduces anxiety and depression while improving your immune system. It helps you think more clearly, make better decisions and boosts your emotional intelligence.[28]

Above all, mindfulness helps you to be more engaged with the present moment. One of the most fascinating studies into the benefits of this was undertaken at Harvard in 2010 by Matt Killingsworth and Dan Gilbert.[29] Using an iPhone App the researchers followed over 2000 volunteers to track their happiness throughout the day. They found that the volunteers were thinking about the past or future, or what they call 'mind-wandering' for 46.9 per cent of their waking time. Entitled 'A Wandering Mind is an Unhappy Mind' the study concluded that being present and absorbed in a task will make you happier, irrespective of the task itself. A wandering mind is the enemy of quality time.

Mindfulness not only helps you enjoy the present moment and think more clearly, it also shifts you from doing and thinking to simply being. You become more aware of the Buddhist notion of impermanence: that you and everything in the world are in a continuous state of flux. Every thought and feeling, every image and sound comes and goes, and you must not attach to any of them. Just observe the sensations as they occur and let go of any judgment.

When you do this you are free. You are free to choose your thoughts and feelings in the moment, whatever is happening around you, whoever and wherever you are. You will let go of many fears and troubles. Maybe, at last, you will realise that this moment is perfect as it is. This is wisdom that we all need to remember.

slow down to pay attention

One of the most effective ways to be more mindful is to slow down and live for the moment. Phil slows down and entrains to the rhythm of life in Punxsutawney. I recommend that you slacken your pace too. If you are constantly busy, rushing around trying to achieve a series of goals, you will always be out of sync with the present moment.

When you slow down you are able to recognise and then disrupt automatic patterns. This is because so much of what you do is at high speed. Most of your behaviour is governed by your habits as you work on autopilot and multitask your way through a hectic schedule.

You can be composing an email while holding a hands-free telephone conversation, making notes for your next meeting and looking around at your colleagues. You are working at such a frenetic pace that you have to rely on short cuts and habitual behaviours just to get through the day. Moreover, the faster you live, the stronger these expedients become, even if they are not serving you in the long run.

At work, at school, and at home we are infatuated with the compulsive urge to fill every moment with activities. Nowhere is this more worrying than with respect to our children. I remember a family where the parents organised every minute of their children's lives like a military campaign. Overscheduled and overstimulated, the poor youngsters were caught in an activity trap, living at a frenzied pace with no room for quiet, unstructured time. Under constant pressure, lacking concentration and uncomfortable with their own company, they suffered from chronic stress and anxiety.

It can sometimes be hard to slow down in today's fast-paced lifestyle, but you can always walk a little slower, take time to notice the sights and sounds around you and not act on every impulse to do more. After a while, you will move out of high-speed autopilot mode and observe what is going on around you, rather than playing out what is going on in your head. It's like what happens when you go on holiday: typically, you continue in work mode for the first few days and then, as you slow down, you think and feel differently. You are more aware of your body, of other people and of your surroundings. For a few days, this feeling of dislocation might be challenging and unnerving. Then, as you gradually awaken from your daily trance and start to pay attention, you begin to enjoy the new sensations.

When you decelerate, you can feel your stress dissolve as you go with the flow. And as you become more relaxed, you realise how tense and tight you were before. You had become accustomed to feeling on edge, as though it was your normal state. A similar thing happens when you are ill and forced to stay in bed. After some initial resistance, you have to accept your situation and naturally slow down. Then your mind and body can relax and heal.

Fortunately, you can bring this relaxed holiday mood into your life whenever and wherever you want. You just need to perform at a gentler pace. Walk more slowly and talk more slowly. Take time for meals and find hobbies that absorb you. Plan a hike at the weekend, perhaps, so that you can take time to pay attention to Nature.

Finding time to stop thinking, to stop doing and to start being is crucial. Only then can you liberate yourself from the incessant demands of your Conditioned Self and its insatiable appetite for activity, achievements and recognition. And only then can you create the time and the space for genuine change.

Instead of setting goals for next year or even for next week, set a goal for the next minute or the next second, and make that goal to be happy now. Focus on the quality of the present moment, not the anticipated rewards in the future. Be mindful for one minute, and then another. Take small steps and notice how it feels to experience the passage of time, minute by minute. Stop making grand plans, and try making small, incremental changes instead. This is how you transform the quality of your life, one minute at a time.

awakening

When Phil arrives in Punxsutawney, he is not paying attention to anything other than his own needs. This is his fourth festival in the town and, for him, the celebrations are nothing more than the backdrop to an irritating chore. On his first day, he does not notice the people or the events around him. He is in such a rush that he steps into a deep puddle by mistake – and does it again the next day. He is trapped in the Groundhog Day Condition even before he is trapped in the time loop itself.

Phil awakens by becoming aware that he is trapped, and then taking action to escape by becoming fully present. You can do the same, when you begin to experience the present moment and stop living in your head, dwelling on the past or future. Remember that the more time you can be present and aware, the happier you will be.[30]

the joy of staying in one place

All men's miseries derive from not being able to sit in a quiet room alone.[31]
Blaise Pascal, French physicist and philosopher

One of the most important insights from *Groundhog Day* is the benefit of staying in one place. At first, Phil hates being stuck in Punxsutawney. As he evolves, he deepens his connection to the town and realises that staying in one place sets him free. Phil has to be confined to fixed boundaries of time and place to dissolve his emotional and psychological boundaries. By ending his travels, he finally arrives.

This has been one of the most valuable lessons in my life too. Previously, whenever I felt down I would distract myself with ideas of escape, and I regularly acted on this impulse. I was restless and impatient. In the space of twenty years I moved house twelve times, obtained a visa to move to New Zealand and even went to live in the US. I started three separate businesses in a year and never focused on any of them. Each was a temporary diversion to keep my mind occupied, and while I loved setting them up, I got bored quickly and moved on. I was addicted to the thrill of the start-up phase, but could not follow through and, of course, they all failed! I became an expert at shifting my attention away from the present moment. At the time it felt normal, as it was my default mode. Looking back, however, I am shocked by my manic behaviour.

Today, I still get agitated. I regularly feel a strong urge to escape, but I am learning to manage this feeling. Now I am able to spend a lot more time enjoying my place. I work from home and spend an hour each day walking in the village and surrounding countryside. When I feel low, I stay put and don't run off. Instead, I switch from doing to being mode. By being immersed in my place and in the now, I have become more aware and also calmer. It is very grounding.

The paradox of staying in one place to be free is an example of the enduring wisdom of *Groundhog Day*. Phil grows not by expanding his horizons but by staying firmly rooted in the same place and one time. He remains in the same location and puts his energies into developing his character, rather than enhancing his status. In so doing, he becomes far more self-aware, peeling back more and more layers of his life. The irony is that he finds what he has always been looking for in the last place he expected. By staying in one place he finds hidden treasures such as meaning, purpose, peace of mind and love. The lesson is clear: look for answers within before you look outside. For it is only when you change your inner world that you can be fully engaged with your life. Marcel Proust captures this idea superbly:

> **The real voyage of discovery consists not in seeking new landscapes, but in having new eyes.**[32]

Groundhog Day is a brilliant story of seeing the familiar with new eyes, and of coming to really know it for the first time. So why not consider abandoning the search for novelty and embrace the mundane instead? I used to think that exploring new places was the answer until I realised that it was simply my means of escaping the present moment.

By staying where you are and seeking fulfilment in the here and now, you can embark on a heroic journey like Phil. Try searching within, and consider what you would do when there were no more distractions. Who are you without your roles, responsibilities, thoughts, feelings and activities? Maybe, like Phil, you will discover something extraordinary in the ordinary, as you venture beyond your conditioned responses to life. Maybe you will attain a level of pure consciousness you could only have dreamed of.

SUMMARY

- When you engage with life you will discover many wonderful gifts.

- Quality time is making the best use of how you experience your precious time to lead the life you want.

- Personal transformation begins when you face and accept reality.

- There is no better moment than now. The more you can be present, the happier you will be.

- Happiness depends more on the quality of your inner experience than on your outer life.

- By being mindful you can create moments of peace in your busy life.

- Slowing down and staying in one place can set you free.

- Seeing the world with a fresh perspective is more likely to make you feel fulfilled than always looking to change your circumstances.

CHAPTER FIVE

simple pleasures

There must be more to life than having everything.[33]

Maurice Sendak, author and illustrator

When you stay in one place and are fully present, you begin to be thankful for what you already have, not what you think you want. This brings you to the next stage in engaging with life, which is to be appreciative of the simple pleasures of everyday life.

Time is your most precious commodity, but how well do you use it? It is far more valuable than money, yet so much easier to waste. The quality of your experience will make you far happier than the quantity of your possessions.[34] And experience doesn't have to mean climbing in the Himalayas, snorkelling in the Barrier Reef or going on Safari in Namibia. Watching the sun set, buying bread from your local bakers or visiting an art gallery where admission is free will often make you just as happy as any exotic holiday.

I made a list of my favourite activities and all of them are within the reach of almost anyone in the UK. They include walking in cities (especially London); having a bath; watching TED videos on my laptop; doing Sudoku and crosswords; listening to Radio 4 while eating breakfast; lighting a candle and observing the flame; grinding beans and making fresh coffee; relaxing in the garden and reading a good book; sitting in front of a fire when it is freezing outside; walking down country lanes when the sun is shining through the leaves; watering the plants on a summer's evening; reading the weekend newspapers in bed; hanging out the washing on a windy day (yes, I really love doing this!) and watching *Match of the Day* when I don't know the results.

Why not make your own list below? Just think of those simple pleasures that make you happy and cost little or nothing.

1

2

3

4

5

6

7

8

9

10

Having lived a life of luxury in my forties, I am now focused on living simply. I have learned that I need very little other than appreciating what I already have. It just requires a change in mindset. To be happy now and for the rest of your life, you need to remove all the conditions you have created that block you: 'I will be happy if I get that raise . . . when I meet the partner of my dreams . . . when I have paid off the mortgage . . . when I can afford to be a full-time musician.' Start from the premise that you need nothing more than you already have for life to be complete.

Phil is a 'glass is half-empty kind of guy' when he arrives in Punxsutawney, and for most of his time there he feels incomplete. He sees the downside of everything – he is stuck in a town he despises with people he has nothing but contempt for; everyone else is having a great time, enjoying the festival. So why is Phil so unhappy? It is not being stuck in Punxsutawney that makes him that way; it is being stuck in the habitual thinking of his Conditioned Self.

Phil has to be stuck in time and place for year after year to learn not to fixate on what he doesn't have. When he stops thinking about his predicament, stops reflecting on the past he has lost and the future denied to him, he is able to be present and savour every glorious moment of his one day. He no longer judges it. The weather might be terrible, the ceremony not to his taste and the people strange, but he lives moment to moment and the rest does not matter, as he is fully absorbed in the flow of his immediate experience. He learns the lesson that he already has everything he needs to be happy. And it is only when he realises this – that happiness means being content with what you have, not craving more – that he is free.

You and I have the same natural ability as Phil to see the remarkable in the mundane. We just keep on forgetting. Indeed, I forget more than most, and this has been one of my biggest challenges.

I promise you that if you shift your attention from wanting to appreciating, from desire to gratitude and seeking to simply being, you will be far happier. Our biggest challenge is not that we don't get what we want, but that we don't know how to enjoy and appreciate what we already have. *Groundhog Day* shows us how to make the transition. I recommend that you devote a minute each day to focusing on switching from desire to appreciation, and then increase it gradually to five minutes, fifteen, thirty minutes and then an hour a day, until it becomes a habit.

I know this works from my own experience, from studying three thousand years' worth of philosophical thought and spiritual wisdom and, more recently, from extensive research in the field of positive psychology.[35]

Throughout history, every type of culture has celebrated the gift of life, and rituals are a great way to do this. One of the best examples is the Jewish Sabbath: for one day a week, you stop working and rest instead. You turn off your mobile, computer and TV and do as little as possible other than traditional activities like eating and talking together as a family. Irrespective of religion or belief, the Sabbath is an excellent ritual for all of us to observe as it counteracts our tendency to complain and bemoan our fate. Try taking one day a week to break from your busy routine to appreciate the good things in your life.

And there are other rituals too. Every morning I take a walk and say 'Thank you' aloud three times. I think about what I have, not what I don't have. It's hard, but it's also an invaluable antidote to constant goal setting.

When you really grasp this you can have a complete turnaround. You can focus on what genuinely makes you happy, rather than what you think will make you happy. Phil has such a turnaround when he removes all conditions to being happy, and fully engages with all the joys life has to offer.

The wisdom of *Groundhog Day* provides a wake-up call to engage with the amazing gift of life. It is like someone shaking you out of your stupor, and saying, 'For Heaven's sake – do you realise how lucky you are? You have it all. Be happy now – stop focusing on what you don't have, and focus on what you do have.'

getting off the hedonic treadmill

So why do we fail to appreciate what we have? Why are we not more content? Why are we so restless? The answer lies in the conditioning, circumstances and habits I explained earlier (see p. 39–43) that conspire to keep us in a state of perpetual dissatisfaction. The Groundhog Day Condition produces what Buddhists term 'attachment'. Buddhists believe our fundamental error is that we spend our lives mesmerised by our need for attachments (such as our craving for possessions or status), rather than letting go of them.

Psychologists have called this 'the hedonic treadmill'. This is an illuminating concept that highlights our dilemma. The idea is that you are on a treadmill where you are always running to get to where you want to be, which is the feeling of pleasure or hedonism. Your challenge is that you continually adapt to whatever you think will make you happy. So, if you double your salary next year, you will feel great for a few days or maybe weeks, if you are lucky. Then you will get used to the new salary and get back on the treadmill, as you want to double it again. This could go on until you are earning £10 million a year, but it will never end. You will always be on the treadmill, wanting more.

I know this feeling all too well myself, and I also know that the treadmill is not just about consumerism and wealth. It is also about the constant search for novel experiences and accomplishments in a bid to escape a persistent sense of emptiness. I have lost so much time in this fruitless search, and I have learned that when you go down this road, whatever you achieve, whatever you acquire, whatever your standing, it will never be enough. Sometimes, the acquisition of status and money are no more than a futile attempt to compensate for not liking yourself. That was true for me: I kept on earning and striving in a vain effort to make up for low self-esteem. To others, my life seemed perfect. I knew that it was deeply flawed.

Whether you are on minimum wage or you are a billionaire, you cannot get off the treadmill if you look outside of yourself to find joy and fulfilment. You just keep on adapting, like an addict looking for their next fix. You may seem to be moving forward, but you are just going from one desire to another, never fully satisfied. Stop for a moment and consider the possibility that getting everything you ever wanted could soon turn into a nightmare as it did for Phil. How does that feel?

At its heart, *Groundhog Day* is a story of two journeys. The outer journey consists of horizontal growth – new places, new people, more acquisitions and more accomplishments. It is a never-ending journey without a destination – because as soon as you think you have arrived, you want to be somewhere else. You become locked in to an unrelenting pursuit of novelty that prevents you from enjoying what you have. Life becomes a zero-sum game where continuously winning and progressing becomes the unattainable goal. Staying in one place directs Phil towards the second type of journey, an inner journey, when the outer one becomes unavailable to him.

Most of what you think will make you happy does not. Material gain is less satisfying, and expected loss less unsatisfactory.[36] If you always want more, if you are always envious of your friend's holidays, houses, car and lifestyles, you will rarely be content. Life will never be good enough, and you will never be satisfied. Of course, there is nothing wrong with self-improvement, but just take care not to become obsessive. Instead, consider committing more time and effort to appreciating the improvements you have already made.

It's vital to remember what is most important. Ceaseless searching and striving prevent you from engaging with your life. You have, within you, an unchanging state of wellbeing that exists irrespective of pleasure or pain, fortune or misfortune. There is a profound source of joy available to you beyond the gratification of your desires and the trials and tribulations you face each day. It is always there, waiting for you to engage with it – and the entry point lies in the present moment.

The inner journey is not travelling to new places. It is travelling deeper within yourself, exploring your inner landscape. It means understanding what really motivates you and what you are really looking for. You can improve the quality of your experience without leaving your room or changing your circumstances. You can embark on this journey whatever age you are, wherever you live and whoever you are. It is the journey of self-discovery. It will change you for ever and, in so doing, will improve the quality of your outer journeys too.

Living for the future is seductive, but it's an unfulfilling refuge from the reality of the present moment. You exchange dealing with the great challenges of your life for the delusion of a brighter future, dependent on constantly searching for something or somebody to rescue you. But only you can rescue yourself, and it starts by challenging your desires.

Like Phil, you may discover that something remarkable occurs when you change your focus from what is missing in your life, and trying always to meet your own needs, to the simple pleasures of everyday life and how you can fulfil the needs of others.

Where is your focus? What if you started tomorrow with the assumption that you already have a perfect life, but just hadn't realised it yet? What if you didn't need anything else? What would it be like to give up all your desires and all your goals? Maybe you don't need any more money, possessions or achievements to be happy. Maybe you don't need anything else at all to complete you. You are complete already.

two bucket lists

Here is a simple exercise to illustrate how a perfect life is already within your grasp, and help you to focus on the benefits of the wonderful inner journey that is available to each of us. You may have already made a 'bucket list' of places you want to visit and activities you want to do before you die. If you have not done it before, write one out now. It could include things like seeing the Grand Canyon, buying a second home by the sea, going on safari in Kenya, writing a book or learning to paint. Now, write a second bucket list that lays out the feelings and inner experiences you want to have. This could include feeling peaceful, a sense of wellbeing, self-esteem or passion.

Your outer bucket list	Your inner bucket list

The first list identifies what you want in your outer life – your *instrumental goals*, such as possessions or activities. The second identifies what you want in your inner life – the feelings and state of mind you desire or your *terminal goals*. When you look at both lists you may notice that the first is designed to produce the feelings and state of mind that you want in the second: you want to go to the Grand Canyon, for example, to feel a sense of awe and wonder, yet this is available to you now when you look up at the sky or take a walk in the park; you want to buy a second home by the sea as a place to relax and get away from it all, yet this is available to you now when you practise mindfulness or do yoga.

You don't have to travel the world or have the perfect outer life to enjoy a gratifying inner life. So why not put your energies into creating that inner life now, rather than delaying it for another second. You can keep the first list – it may enhance your life, but it will never replace the second list. Because isn't that what you want more than anything?

Ultimately, we all want to experience a set of feelings. These will vary, though most of us want the feeling of loving and being loved, of security and inner peace, of having a greater purpose, of connection and of being liked and appreciated. And we want those feelings more than the specific achievement or possession that we believe will produce them.

the miracle of your life

There are two ways to live: you can live as if nothing is a miracle; you can live as if everything is a miracle.[37]

Albert Einstein, physicist

Your life is already miraculous. It is just your thinking and attitudes that conceal this. Perhaps the best way to be more appreciative is to contemplate the miracle of your life: the odds of being born at all are incalculable.[38] If you won the National Lottery every week for a lifetime, you would still not come close to the odds of being born. So why not follow Einstein's advice and celebrate the gift of your life with the same excitement as a lottery winner.

Your body consists of trillions of cells all working in harmony to look after you and give you the gift of consciousness. What material possessions can compete with that? Whatever you accomplish in your lifetime, nothing will even come close to the glorious gift of life. If you can just acknowledge this gift every day, and practise gratitude in everything you do, you will engage with the miracle of your life and be far happier than you would be on the hedonic treadmill, forever seeking your next fix.

Whenever you feel dissatisfied or resentful, just focus on the marvel of your birth. Here is a practice that might help:

Appreciate Your Ancestors

Find a quiet place where you can be on your own, take a deep breath and think about your parents. Picture them when they were young and think about how they met. Now think about the odds of them meeting, coming together and your mother giving birth to you. Yes, that particular sperm made it through to fertilise your mother's egg. The chances of you being born are trillions to one against – yet you made it! Now I would like you to say thank you to them. Thank them for giving you the gift of life.

Now think about your grandparents and repeat the same process. Picture them as young people meeting, coming together and producing your mum and dad. Thank them too. Now think of your great-grandparents, then their parents and the thousands of ancestors who survived and procreated to give you the gift of life. Imagine a procession of all the people responsible for your life going back over the millennia. Look at them all and say, 'Thank you, thank you, thank you!'

If you do this exercise repeatedly, I challenge you to feel dissatisfied, sad or bitter. I dare you to tell me that you cannot be happy now or that you still need that big mansion, that sports car, that perfect wedding to feel complete. Listen to your ancestors, as they implore you with one resounding voice to savour every moment of your precious time!

MY GRANDFATHERS

I have always struggled to be grateful, but a few years ago I learned of an extraordinary event in my own past that changed everything.

My father served in the British Navy in the Second World War and his father served in the army in the First World War. My grandfather was called Thomas. He worked for WHSmith in London before the war, and on 8 August 1915 he arrived at Gallipoli for one of the most infamous military campaigns in British history that cost Churchill his job as Naval Secretary. Much worse, however, there were over 200,000 British casualties and my grandfather contracted dysentery and was critically ill. He never fully recovered from the illness or the experience, and had a lifetime of medical problems.

On the very same day that Thomas arrived at Gallipoli, my maternal grandfather, Henry, did too. He was from Lancashire and served in a different regiment, yet they were both plunged into this nightmare at exactly the same time. And, just like Thomas, Henry nearly died. He was shot in the head, and lost an eye.

Yet both survived. They made it back to the UK and both got married. Eight years after Gallipoli, within the space of just nine days, Thomas became the proud father of Roy and Henry became the proud father of Mary. Roy and Mary then met twenty-five years later and married in 1952. Seven years later they gave birth to their only child – Paul Hannam.

I am writing these words in November 2014, a few days after visiting the poppies at the Tower of London commemorating the 100th anniversary of the Great War. I thanked both my grandfathers for their sacrifices a century ago, and for their legacy. For whenever I feel depressed or disappointed, or whenever I feel that life is not fair, I think of the two of them and imagine them marching past each other in opposite directions, and exchanging the briefest of smiles. Then I thank them and also my late father and my mother for giving me life.

what are you going to do with the gift of life?

Remembering who you are, and where you came from can really help when it comes to making a commitment to treasure life and not take it for granted.

To bring this message home I want to turn to another film, the magnificent *Saving Private Ryan*. Near the end, there is a scene that is among the most moving I have ever watched. Captain John Miller, played by Tom Hanks, is mortally wounded, having undertaken a dangerous mission after D-Day to save Private Ryan, played by Matt Damon. He has already lost most of his men in the rescue and, seconds from death, Captain Miller pulls Ryan towards him and utters his very last words: 'Earn this.'

The final scene of the film finds Ryan forty years later, visiting Miller's grave in Normandy. Shaking with emotion, he asks his wife to confirm that he has led a good life, and that he is a 'good man' who is deserving of the terrible sacrifice that Miller and his men made. He then salutes the grave, reminding me of my father, my grandfathers and all the people who overcame terrible adversity to give *me* the gift of life.

One of the most sobering and liberating questions is to ask yourself, as Ryan did, 'Have I earned my life?' You do not have to be a saint or discover a cure for cancer. No, the point is whether you have made the most of the life you have been given.

Appreciate what you have today. Let death be the great teacher now, and don't wait until your final hours. Eastern traditions encourage you to contemplate your death, so that you may better understand your life. If you imagine lying on your deathbed and considering your current problems, they will probably seem a lot less important. Allow yourself to be happier by letting go of your desires and fears, and appreciating what is truly important. It makes sense not to wait until your last days on earth to grasp this.

In her book, *Regrets of the Dying*, Bronnie Ware describes her extensive experience working in a hospice. She lists five regrets of the people she cared for, and the final one is perhaps the most poignant: 'I wish that I had let myself be happier.'[39]

The words 'let myself be happier' are important, as you already have a great capacity for happiness. You just need to let yourself be happy by making a decision to be happy above all else. You have a natural facility for joy that is always available. Just as a beautiful plant needs to be rid of the weeds that are choking it so that it can bloom, you need to clear your own emotional weeds so that your Authentic Self can blossom.

savour each moment

Understandably, in the beginning of *Groundhog Day* Phil only sees the nightmare of his predicament. When he starts to pay attention though, he becomes aware of the enchanting nature of ordinary small-town life. Punxsutawney turns out to be a delightful town of decent people, each of whom has their own value. He begins to relish the mundane sequence of daily events, the prosaic content of each conversation and the simple stories of everyone he meets. He relishes the charm and beauty of the commonplace, stops lamenting what he has lost and takes pleasure instead in what he has now. Playing the piano at a local concert becomes more fun than a sophisticated nightlife.

Phil fundamentally alters his perspective of time. He stops thinking about being stuck and starts to savour the time he has. He narrows his focus to the immediate which broadens his awareness. Put simply, Phil learns to savour his life, and this is the ideal way to be appreciative and grateful. You may have everything you ever wanted. You may have travelled to the four corners of the world, accomplished every goal you set out to and become the envy of all your friends. Yet how well have you savoured the moments of your journey. How long did the joy of each pinnacle and peak experience last?

Savouring is deliberately noticing and acknowledging all that is good in your life. It is taking longer to eat a meal, to listen to a friend or watch a sunset. It is slowing down and being attentive to all the many small pleasures you previously ignored or overlooked. Savouring is also the ability to make these positive feelings longer-lasting and more intense, by being more mindful. This is an invaluable natural ability that you already possess. When you savour each moment you are fully engaging with life.

Groundhog Day illustrates clearly the difference between squandering and valuing your time each day. You are offered a life-changing choice in every moment: to select the path of engaging or disengaging. And every second, every minute, every hour and every day of your life that you are not savouring is wasted time.

Phil has to lose everything to realise that he is already rich. It is often the case that only when you lose something are you able to appreciate it. For example, last year I had an operation on my knee and could not walk more than a few steps for eight weeks. When I took my first proper walk outside, I felt boundless joy. There are millions of people who do not enjoy this capability, and one day I may not be able to walk either. So for now I try to be grateful for each step.

Whatever you earn, whatever you achieve, it all pales into insignificance compared to the wonder of movement, sight, hearing, speech, smell, taste and touch. Many are denied one or more of these, and they will usually appreciate those senses they do have far more as a result.

This is exemplified by the remarkable Helen Keller who was struck with blindness and deafness from the age of one, and went on to publish twelve books and become one of the most extraordinary women in history. Her intention was to savour every moment and make the best of all the gifts she still enjoyed. Her belief was that 'Life is either a daring adventure, or nothing'.[40]

So, whatever suffering you are enduring, make sure that you find time to take stock of what is positive. We often savour the simple pleasures of life when we experience contrast. So when you have been out in the freezing cold, sitting in front of a warm fire is delightful. When you are exhausted, sleep is exquisite. Think of when you last had a toothache and how every waking hour was dominated by the nagging, relentless pain. Then, recall the ecstasy as the pain stopped.

Psychologists have proven the value of savouring in sustaining happiness, so why not make it your priority?[41]

remembering you are happy already

Here is a question for you to ponder: what if you were already happy, but did not know it? Let's say everything is going your way right now – you have a job you like, a rewarding relationship, an enjoyable social life. You have no big health problems or financial worries. Well, why are you not happier?

Maybe you have adapted to your happiness. Just like you tend to take your physical health for granted until you are ill or in pain, maybe you also take your emotional wellbeing for granted until you are sad or stressed. I have an old friend, who is in her eighties, and she always tells me to enjoy being young because it is no fun getting old and infirm. She suffers from arthritis and other conditions that cause constant discomfort. Her highest points are when her pain is at its lowest. So her illnesses structure and determine the quality of life. She handles them very well, yet would give anything to be able to go back to when she was forty-five and tell her younger self to enjoy and appreciate being healthy instead of dwelling on trivial issues like traffic jams or irritating neighbours.

Now, imagine you are in your nineties and suffering from a debilitating illness. What would the older you say to the you who is reading these words now? Would they say, 'Work harder, get more anxious, make more money, set more goals and win the approval of more people?' Or would the older you say, 'I beg you to savour each moment of your life and be grateful that you are healthy and happy now. You do not need anything else or to be anyone else. Just relish the life you have.'

You have to choose to be happy. Your happiness results less from positive events than from a positive attitude. There will be good fortune in your life. You may live to a hundred or enjoy a long and loving marriage. The question is how well you relish your good fortune when it occurs. Happiness is a skill. So maybe it's time to spend more time savouring the good things in your life, and less time resenting what you don't have or craving more

This is why savouring is so critical. It is not what is happening that counts. It is how you are experiencing what is happening. To illustrate this, I want to tell you about a walk I took across London Bridge in the early-morning rush hour. It was a beautiful autumnal day. The sun was shining, and the air was crisp. I observed maybe a hundred people. Some were walking towards me, some to the side and some were overtaking me. Most were walking purposefully, focused on getting to work on time and possibly planning the day ahead. Many were talking on their phones, texting, browsing or listening to music. Some people look resigned, others dejected. None of them looked particularly content and no one was looking about them at the majestic London skyline. Nobody seemed aware of the glorious weather or grateful to be working in one of the greatest cities on the planet. Everyone was lost in their thoughts, disconnected from the spectacle of life around them.

Watching the behaviour of commuters during the rush hour is eye-opening. It is proof of the Groundhog Day Condition at work and demonstrates our difficulty in taking pleasure in what we have. It is a classic example of means and ends. Most commuters see time spent in traffic or on a busy train as wasted time – a grind that has to be endured. The thinking goes like this: I have to commute for two hours each day, so I can get to work for forty hours a week, so I can earn enough money to survive and hopefully do the things that make me happy. Happiness, for them, is the anticipated reward for all that time and effort. A few hours of pleasure in exchange for fifty hours of sacrifice!

Now let me suggest an alternative. Instead of viewing your commute as something to be tolerated so you might be happy, why not decide to be happy during your commute. Why delay the feelings you want? It won't be easy, as it probably means changing a deeply ingrained habit, but why not commit to improving the quality of your experience? What if you could be as happy in heavy traffic on a damp Monday morning as you are with your friends at the pub on a Friday evening? If you can crack that, you will open the door to enjoying every moment of your life. For changing a keystone habit like the way you think and feel about commuting will trigger other positive changes in your life.

You may think that commuting is a necessary evil or a means to an end and is, therefore, a poor example. Yet is it so different from much of your time at work or even at home? How much of your other activity is also a means to an end?

Try keeping a journal for one day and write down where your attention is focused. Set a timer on your phone to remind you to stop every hour to record your entries, and always bring it back to savouring what is good. It may be simply appreciating your breathing or even your ability to write. Observe and celebrate your 'aliveness' whenever you can. Every time you stop to count your blessings, you are reminding yourself that you are, in fact, already happy.

appreciation comes from within

When you focus on trying to improve your inner experience, you will be more appreciative and more content. Phil struggles with this, feeling profoundly disengaged and even desolate.

It is important not to buy into all the marketing and advertising that tell you what you are lacking. Modern consumer society depends on your perpetual dissatisfaction. You are encouraged to buy products to help fill the gaps in your life. The problem is that no purchase ever does that for more than a passing moment, and so you become ensnared in a never-ending cycle of dissatisfaction and consumerism. You need only turn on the TV and watch the commercials for fitness equipment, diet pills and baldness cures to see what I mean – thousands of commercials and they all have one message: you will only be happy when you have bought this product.

But when you stop using your external life as a measure for feeling good about yourself, you will discover that your inner life is the answer. You don't need more possessions, wealth or power so much as you need more awareness. Shift your focus from seeking new experiences to improving the quality of your current one: notice the falling leaves in your garden now, rather than waiting until you can see the fall in New England. Life is happening in front of you. You do not need to be anywhere else.

counting your blessings

If you want to spend more time dwelling on the positive and on simple pleasures, I recommend that you keep a 'gratitude journal', in which you write down three specific things to be grateful for every day. It might be a good conversation with a friend or a funny video that made you laugh out loud; it may be that you noticed the sound of a songbird or the first daffodils bursting into flower; it can even be taking a shower, eating breakfast or that first sip of coffee in the morning. Why not start this practice right away:

1

2

3

A gratitude journal is savouring in practice. Every time you write down something good that has occurred you are building appreciation. Every time you stop to count your blessings, you are reminding yourself that you are already content. This also means that you appreciate yourself. Stop fixating on what you have not done or what you think you ought to be doing, and reflect on how far you have come. Stop disliking yourself, and like yourself for who you are – warts and all.

The Greater Good Science Centre at the University of California, Berkeley, one of the world's leading academic institutions, studies the psychology, sociology and neuroscience of wellbeing, and teaches skills for fostering a resilient and compassionate society. Their work includes a multi-million-dollar research project into the benefits of gratitude.[42]

They are building on research that shows that people who practise gratitude regularly:

- have stronger immune systems and lower blood pressure
- have higher levels of positive emotions
- have more joy, optimism and happiness
- tend to display more generosity and compassion
- feel less lonely and isolated.

If all you do as a result of reading this book is to start keeping a gratitude journal and shift more of your attention to what you have rather than what you don't have, you will already be happier. Gratitude is the direct route to a better quality of life.

a simple life

When you are grateful you do not need as much to be happy. What seemed so important before become less so, as you enjoy the good life you have here and now. Like Phil, you may begin to simplify your life and reduce everything to the essence of what really matters, peeling away the layers that obscure your Authentic Self. And then you will realise that taking a walk, feeling the sun on your face or holding the hand of a loved one are unimaginably superior to any sports car, luxury home or expensive cruise.

You might think at first that the simple things are the opposite of what you want. Phil certainly does. Yet he eventually grasps that the ultimate choice is, in the words of American author, speaker and educator Duane Elgin, a 'way of life that is outwardly simple, inwardly rich'.[43]

Phil transforms his life by needing less. He becomes more content moving from the big city to the small town; from the high-pressure career to a slower pace; from complexity to simplicity. He discovers that the best things in life are free. In Punxsutawney he owns very little; instead, he finds pleasure in art, authentic relationships and being part of a community. He focuses his energy on significance not success, on his wellbeing not his wealth and on his personal growth not his personal status.

Phil goes back to basics, and so can you. What does a simple life mean to you? Does it mean working fewer hours, living in a smaller house, buying less stuff or decluttering your home? For me, a simple life means spending as much of my valuable time as possible on the activities that I am passionate about.

So, why not try spending less time managing your career and finances, and more time managing your expectations? After all, it is your expectations and aspirations that make you frustrated, not lack of wealth or status. When you are running on the hedonic treadmill, you may be financially wealthy but 'time-poor'.

Are you so fixated on the clouds passing by that you do not see that the sun is always there just behind? Only when you simplify your life will you be able to see beyond the clouds that have obscured your vision and kept you in the dark. And that's when you'll realise that you are whole already.

Let your future be a story of reduction not accumulation. When you go back to basics, you can reshape your life on the building blocks of what matters most to you. You can choose to lead a simple life that creates the time and space to improve the standard of your experience, rather than your standard of living. When you discard the trivial, you are better able to spend your days wisely. You do not need to live in a cave or give away everything. You just need to find a better balance or follow what Buddhism and Daoism define as the Middle Way.[44]

The Middle Way means avoiding extremes, and I have found this an incredibly valuable principle. Let's say you are confronted by a drunk in the street who asks for money. Your natural reaction may be to go to one of two extremes: fight or flight. You may shout at the drunk and get angry or walk rapidly to the other side of the street to avoid them. But there is always an alternative which is to opt for a more balanced response. In this case, it may mean simply smiling, saying 'No' and walking on with your head held high.

The Middle Way can be applied to all areas of our lives: with diet, there is a middle way between gluttony and fasting; with exercise, there is a middle way between doing none and over-exercising; at work there is a middle way between ignoring your colleagues or trying to please each one of them all the time. When we put the Middle Way into action we transcend our initial impulses and conditioned responses, and make more measured and considered choices. This, in turn, helps us to live more authentically, and less on autopilot, which liberates us from the Groundhog Day Condition.

Most of all, you need to decide what is of greatest importance to you and recognise that you are part of a culture that pressures you again and again to buy more, have more and do more. You may need to swim against the material tide of our culture, but the reward can be life changing. Another one of the five regrets of the dying mentioned earlier (and the one expressed by almost everyone) was, 'I wish I didn't work so hard'.[45]

The most valuable asset of a material life is money, but the most valuable asset of a simple life is time. Maybe it is time to alter your perception of value, reorder your priorities and set out in a new direction. Take this opportunity to redefine what the good life means to you. All you need is time.

grace with your presence

One of the most inspiring invocations of how to live is found at the beginning of another film, *The Tree of Life* – a beautiful, haunting film about a family in 1950s America. Early on, the mother recalls her religious education:

The nuns taught us there are two ways through life, the way of Nature and the way of Grace. You have to choose which one you'll follow. Grace doesn't try to please itself. Accepts being slighted, forgotten, disliked. Accepts insults and injuries . . . Nature only wants to please itself. Get others to please it too. Likes to lord it over them. To have its own way. It finds reasons to be unhappy when all the world is shining around it. And love is smiling through all things . . . The nuns taught us that no one who loves the way of grace ever comes to a bad end.[46]

The Tree of Life, Terrence Malick

I find this truly inspiring. I want nothing to disturb my state of grace; I never want to let my mood be dependent on whether I get what I want or not; and I never want to postpone feeling good until conditions are just so. You will feel amazing when you sustain a state of grace irrespective of what happens to you.

You do not have to be religious to live this way – I am certainly not. If you prefer, you can replace the word 'grace' with 'appreciation' or 'gratitude', but the critical point is this: do you want to live the way of grace or the way of Nature? Do you want to be happy or find reasons to be unhappy?

Phil shifts from living the way of Nature to the way of grace, and you can follow his lead. When you live in a state of grace you engage with the majesty of being alive, and are conscious of just how fortunate you are. Grace turns your conditioning on its head. When you live this way, everything flows smoothly. All moments are significant moments and everything is sacred.

When you live in grace, you are at a higher level of consciousness. You are more aware of who you really are, and of the fact that you are much more than your habits, moods or impulses. Grace is the highest form of living as you fully engage with the moment-to-moment rhythm of being alive. Grace awakens your innate wellbeing, appreciation and wisdom to the benefit of you and everyone whom you 'grace with your presence'.

In a state of grace, all that matters to you is this moment. Achievement, acclaim and prestige mean little. You feel only love for everything and everyone around you. Outcomes, results and worldly pleasures fade into insignificance. The sheer pleasure of being alive is reward enough.

You do not have to withdraw from the world to experience this way of being. You just need to commit to fully engaging with the moment-to-moment unfolding of your life. When you do, you will lose nothing and gain everything.

Even if you have worldly goals, you are more likely to achieve success by maintaining a harmonious, appreciative inner state. You do not need to feel angry, dissatisfied or resentful to motivate yourself. To paraphrase Helen Keller, you should be happy with what you have while working for what you want. Whatever you choose, spend more time on being happy with what you have and less on working for what you want. Our culture has got it so wrong: there is far too much emphasis on our wants, and not nearly enough on appreciation. And it is time to redress the balance.

I believe that there is nothing more important than maintaining a feeling of gratitude for as much of your day as possible, whatever drama or crises are happening around you. Never let anything disturb your state of Grace.

Only you can make yourself happy, only you can engage with your life and only you can improve the quality of your experience of this moment. So why not stop trying to change your outer life to give you the feelings you want? They are already there waiting. You just have to let go of your Conditioned Self and enjoy the simple pleasures of life.

SUMMARY

- The best things in life are available to most of us, and cost little or nothing.

- Rituals help us to be more aware of the extraordinary gift of our ordinary lives.

- Get off the hedonic treadmill and appreciate what you have. Life is a miracle so savour every precious moment.

- Like Phil, focus on the inner journey; he escapes his Conditioned Self and so can you.

- Appreciate and savour every moment. Gratitude is proven to boost your wellbeing in every area of your life.

- Live simply and enjoy the simple pleasures.

- Remember to live in a state of grace every day.

CHAPTER SIX

meet your authentic self

> **I'm not going to live by their rules anymore.**
>
> Phil Connors, *Groundhog Day*

The quality of our lives is determined by the rules that we have chosen to live by. Usually, we are unaware of these rules, such as the attitudes, norms and conditioning that influence us. We are, to a large degree, disengaged from ourselves. In this chapter, you will learn how to be more self-aware and to engage with yourself – your Authentic Self. You can follow a similar path to Phil, and achieve your full potential for growth.

You might know what you want to achieve, and where you want to live. But how often do you think about who you want to be? I have difficulty answering this question. One of my biggest challenges is flipping back and forth between two competing identities; between my Conditioned and Authentic Self.

My Conditioned Self is the 'material me', the sum of my achievements, qualifications, possessions, wealth, knowledge and status. It is my personality and my roles. My Authentic Self is the 'non-material me'. And I'm not talking about a religious state. I mean something simpler and universal here. I believe that you and I have an 'Authentic Self' that is who we are beyond our trappings, like our appearance, education and so on. It is stable and unwavering, impervious to life's ups and downs. It is a deep inner awareness that is ever present, regardless of what is going on in our outer lives. It is our character and values, and is completely separate from position or status.

Our Conditioned and Authentic Selves are not exact, measurable states of mind. They are two ends of a spectrum and we shift back and forth between them all the time. My aim is not to be perfect, but to be my Authentic Self as much as possible and stop slipping back into my Conditioned Self.

Your Authentic Self is the part of you hidden by your Conditioned Self. When you are more self-aware, you are clearer on what is most important. As you see beyond your conditioning, you are better able to understand and integrate your values, thoughts and actions. This is living with integrity and what I mean by engaging with yourself.

The alternative is that you continue to define yourself by the circumstances or the content of your life, such as your job, your marriage, your parental role, education, age or gender. If you do this, you are blocking a deeper and broader version of yourself that is free of the limiting beliefs and habits developed since childhood.

For Phil, it is only when he loses everything that he finds himself. He has to disengage completely from his previous life to fully engage with his potential. He has to lose his independence, his power, his status and the old life that he had been accustomed to. He has to lose time itself. In essence, he disengages from his Conditioned Self and engages with his Authentic Self

Your Authentic Self is not an ideal state. You can never be perfect or be held accountable to unattainable standards. Your behaviour, moods and state of mind vary like the wind, and it can sometimes feel like you alter your personality based on who you are with, how you feel and many other physical, emotional and social factors. Yet, despite the impact of these transitory influences, I believe that you have a discernibly higher, or better, self that needs to be nurtured. I believe that when you are still and present, you are more aware that you have the choice to be authentic or not, to be honest or in denial, to be loving or selfish.

Your Authentic Self is a direction to aim for, a point on a compass that helps you know if you are moving forward or backward. It is a sense that you are doing the right thing, and being true to yourself and your convictions, not being self-serving or trying to please others all the time. Often, this is an intuition that you are doing, or not doing, what you were meant to.

Phil is forced to become self-aware. There is no hiding place in Punxsutawney. Under the fierce spotlight of his plight,

Phil's facade crumbles. His ego and narcissism are shattered. He loses everything to discover what really matters. Once he acknowledges that nothing changes in the outer world, he is able to discern his inner patterns more clearly. Your challenge is to recognise these patterns in a world when they might otherwise remain unnoticed, as you are so busy running from one activity to another.

How self-aware are you? How do you want to spend your time and are you clear about the meaning of your life? I'm not talking about what you own, what you do for a living or what you have achieved. In the film, Phil strips down to the essence of his identity. Following a long tradition going back to Buddha and even beyond, he discards his material self to reveal his Authentic (and, I believe, his better) Self.

An authentic life is a good life. By the end of the film, Phil is leading a good life, helping others to do the same. He lives by principles that any religion or ethical code would endorse; for a good life is built on ethics and virtues. *Groundhog Day* is a story of character development, and character is comprised of universal virtues such as compassion, resilience, courage, resourcefulness, justice, kindness, integrity and fairness.

When you are disengaged, you are less likely to act in accordance with such virtues as you are less aware, and tend to react to your circumstances rather than follow a set of principles. You are subject to the impact of fluctuating events, personal interactions and, more than anything, you are at the mercy of your moods.

Your moods are cyclical and affect you profoundly. Your personality and whole outlook can alter fundamentally as your moods vary. According to psychologist Robert Thayer, moods are 'more important than daily activities, money, status, and even personal relationships because these things are usually filtered through our moods. In many ways our moods are at the core of our being.'[47]

When you are in a low mood, success and achievement are poor compensation; when you are in an upbeat mood, you can handle whatever trouble is thrown at you. You can observe this at work in *Groundhog Day*, as, to paraphrase Charles Dickens, it is a 'Tale of Two Moods': a negative and a positive mood. Indeed, we can borrow the opening lines of Dickens's book and claim that it was the 'best of times and the worst of times'.

Herein lies the extraordinary power of moods. Phil's circumstances remain the same, but his mood alters his experience fundamentally. It has been both the best of times for Phil and also the worst of times. Moreover, he learns that he has the power to create either: he creates the worst of times when he is locked into his Conditioned Self and acts out of self-interest; he creates the best of times when he fully engages with his Authentic Self, and helps other people with love and compassion.

Your Authentic Self seeks nothing, and is happy with what is. It is complete. Whereas your Conditioned Self looks for answers in your outer life, your Authentic Self looks for them within. It is grounded in the immediate, comfortable with uncertainty, contradiction and paradox. It dwells in stillness, in the space between thought and action. This is where you find true freedom.

engaging with your emotions

When you are still and quiet you engage with yourself, and this means engaging with your emotions. You are able to recognise and stay in touch with your feelings, rather than trying to ignore or avoid them. Once you stop running away from difficult feelings, you are in a better place to grow.

Your Conditioned Self has many support structures, including a series of routine responses such as denial, defensiveness and diversion to keep you stuck at your level of development. You have to be aware of these and break the patterns, by not avoiding the feelings as they arise. Over time, the patterns will weaken, and be replaced by more mature and healthy ones. The solution lies in identifying your emotions and learning to interpret what they mean.

Sometimes these emotions are painful, and you will feel vulnerable. This is healthy. Author Brené Brown believes that our vulnerability is the source for many qualities such as passion, creativity and joy. She encourages us to discard our armour and be vulnerable, so we can open ourselves up to new experiences, new feelings and be more authentic. This, in turn, will make us stronger and more courageous and lead to what she terms 'wholeheartedness':

> **Embracing our vulnerabilities is risky but not nearly as dangerous as giving up on love and belonging and joy—the experiences that make us the most vulnerable. Only when we are brave enough to explore the darkness will we discover the infinite power of our light.**[48]

Phil becomes wholehearted as he is forced to feel vulnerable. Day after day he tries to save the life of a homeless man by providing him with food and shelter. All his attempts fail and he experiences a deep sense of loss when he cannot save the old man, despite his valiant attempts. Wholeheartedness means accepting and even embracing your flaws and your suffering. When you feel your own pain, you are able to feel the pain of others too. This is what makes us human.

engaging with your body

Engaging with yourself also involves physical connection. When was the last time you were in touch with your body? When was the last time you stopped thinking, and noticed how you felt physically? We tend to be lost in thought most of the time, and ignore our bodies until we feel pain. As we rush around, we overlook our physicality. How little we appreciate our amazing bodies that have kept us going for all these years.

Mindfulness, yoga and other practices are vital in helping

147

to re-engage you with your body and enhance your senses. They ground you, making you aware of your energy and how you feel physically at all times. When you are mindful of physical sensations, such as how you are breathing, you move your attention away from mental activity and find a source of calm that is always at your service.

The more you engage with your body, the more relaxed, aware and resilient you will become. You will think and feel more clearly, and also communicate more effectively so that other people will notice that you are more open and present.

Phil changes his physical state over the course of the film, and so can you. Your physical and emotional states are interdependent. If you want to feel more positive, then change your physiology. Stand taller, breathe more deeply and smile more broadly. Even better, go for a brisk walk or a run. Each movement and activity helps to release endorphins and boost your energy, so you can more easily move into your peak state.[49]

engaging with your values

As you become attuned to your body and mind, you should become clearer about your core values. Initially, at best, Phil is disengaged from his own values and, at worst, he is motivated by just the one: self-interest. Over time, he gradually realises what matters most, and aligns his actions to his values.

When you are engaged with your values, you find meaning,

purpose and significance in what you do. The question is, do you know what your values are in the first place – the ones that will guide you? Looking at the list below, highlight the values that resonate most with you, and consider how they are manifested in what you do each day:

Health	Peace	Success
Gratitude	Recognition	Love
Sustainability	Fame	Humour
Competition	Independence	Freedom
Status	Simplicity	Wealth
Kindness	Power	Service
Creativity	Fairness	Respect
Control	Justice	Compassion
Responsibilty	Equality	Creativity
Achievement	Wisdom	Wellbeing
Happiness	Intellect	Excellence

Your values are important. They give your life greater meaning. When you stop thinking about what you want and start thinking about what you stand for, you will be more inspired. If you do not have a reason to get up in the morning, it is difficult to find the energy and optimism to flourish. If you do not have a purpose, you can feel like a rudderless boat, and will tend to float about without direction, dependent on the currents of your circumstances.

Meaning fills the void in our lives. Perhaps the most powerful example of this is found in Victor Frankl's book, *Man's Search for Meaning*. Frankl was a psychiatrist who survived as a prisoner in Auschwitz and other death camps in the Second World War. He believed that our main concern as humans lies 'in fulfilling a meaning and in actualizing values, rather than in the mere gratification and satisfaction of drives and instincts.'[50] He showed that even in the worst predicament imaginable, we have control over our inner life. As long as we find meaning and hope, we can survive.

Your values are essentially beliefs that provide direction and vitality. When you change your beliefs you change everything. We can appreciate the power of beliefs from religion. Religious people tend to be far more content than the rest of us. Studies have shown repeatedly that religious affiliation increases life satisfaction and resilience. The social support and shared beliefs of a congregation are ideal ways to boost wellbeing.[51]

I sometimes wish I could be a believer. Life would be so much easier. In terms of our conditioning, there is no more reassuring and comprehensive set of conditions to live by than a systematic rule-based religion. Every time I go to London I see Jehovah's Witnesses standing outside the tube stations in the City, passing out their leaflets to wealthy bankers. Despite the wide gap in earnings, it is obvious who is more content.

Now you may not have the same convictions as the Jehovah's Witnesses, but what if you had the same intensity of beliefs for something you truly valued. You can live in a state of grace without being religious. I am a card-carrying Humanist, for example, and subscribe to their mission 'to be rational, looking to science in attempting to understand the universe, and ethical, seeking to act in a way that puts human welfare at the centre of morality; and . . . to make meaning in life in the here and now.'[52] I want to live ethically and find 'meaning in life in the here and now'. This is a simple and empowering principle.

Religious beliefs may appear irrational, but are our secular beliefs so very different? Beliefs are not scientific facts. They can never be entirely true. So why not create beliefs and values that are good for you, other people and future generations? Why not choose to have more optimistic, positive and ethical beliefs? What do you have to lose? If neither positive nor negative beliefs are objectively true, then surely it is better to choose ones that make you happier. I am not suggesting that you believe in Santa Claus or join a cult. What I am advocating is that you choose rational, healthy beliefs. These could include the belief that it is just fine if not everybody agrees with you, or that you do not have to be perfect in everything you do. Healthy beliefs are in contrast to unhealthy ones like, 'I am a bad person if someone criticises me', or, 'People will only like me if I am successful'. I know these only too well.

Now this seems obvious yet, in practice, it is hard. I was raised to have a sceptical, even cynical, view of positive thinking. By nature, I am suspicious of people who are always upbeat and optimistic. I believe they are either trying to preach to me, or that they lack intellectual rigour. Instinctively, I would challenge people's rosy world views rather than accept them. For years, I was critical, detached and cynical and just like Phil at the beginning of the film.

As I got older, however, I stopped being so dismissive and judgmental. I realised that I did not know all the answers, and that my self-esteem did not rest on intellectual superiority. Above all, I acknowledged that this was making me unhappy. Over time, I let go of my need to be right or appear clever and developed a far more valuable philosophy based on two central principles:

1. Life is a mystery and I know very little.

2. I am imperfect and often don't practise what I preach.

I try not to take myself as seriously as I used to because I can see the inconsistency, self-deception and disparity that lie between my espoused values and my actual behaviour.

For example, one of my highest values is sustainability, but what does that actually mean in practice? I consume far more resources than the average inhabitant of our planet, so what right do I have to challenge people who live unsustainably?

I also realise that instead of always thinking about myself, it's time to think about what my life should represent. What do I really stand for? What principles do I commit to in terms of my lifestyle, career and actions? Which of my values are non-negotiable? How about you: what does your life represent? What values do you hold dear, and to what extent do you live by them? If you want to achieve genuine transformation, this is a critical question. Your values are the engine that will sustain and drive the 'New You' forward for years to come. Surely then, you should know what values you are prepared to uphold?

When Phil learns what his values are and truly connects to them he achieves an extraordinary breakthrough. This is the essence of engaging to yourself. It is when you decide to take yourself seriously and commit to linking your values to your thoughts and actions. You do not need to be a saint. You just need to choose one or two values that you will seek to apply to future decisions and behaviours without exception. If you choose family, then you might turn down a job that involves a lot of international travel; if you choose simplicity, you might choose to buy a small home, even though you could afford a larger one. Your values should be ethical and give you a new sense of direction and purpose. Then you will be less uncertain and confused, and far clearer about what you should do from now on.

connecting the parts

Engaging with yourself requires that you connect the different parts of your character. In the beginning, Phil is fragmented and disengaged. He is unaware of the values that he adopts until much later. On his final day in Punxsutawney he is fully connected to himself, however, and fully engaged in a life where he values others and feels valued by people who he has developed friendships with. He becomes a whole person, living at the height of his powers.

Becoming fully engaged demands that you connect and align each part of yourself. If parts of you are in conflict – say one part wants to be rich and another wants a simple life – you are weaker; your energy is dispersed in inner conflict and you are split, a divided self. Only when you merge the parts can you be whole.

You are whole when your thoughts, feelings and actions are in harmony. And your values act as a robust and unifying centre at the heart of everything you do. As you align each part, you are able to transcend your Conditioned Self, making you more authentic, as you become who you choose to be not what was chosen for you. You take control and don't let your personal situation or habits dictate your course.

As Phil integrates and aligns each part of his Authentic Self, he strengthens his inner life and this, in turn, improves his outer life. He creates a virtuous circle of thinking, feeling and acting that sustains him at a peak state. This is living life to the full. You feel strong and joyful when you have a clear direction and coherent values to follow.

The film compresses the journey into one intense day, but some people take a lifetime to reach this point, while others never get there at all. In many ways Phil 'reconditions' himself through his trials and tribulations, and when you apply the practices in this book you can do the same. When you finally break free from your Conditioned Self, you will unlock talents, motivation and energy that may have been dormant for years. This is the promise of becoming your Authentic Self.

> **If you deliberately plan to be less than you are capable of being, then I warn you that you'll be deeply unhappy for the rest of your life.**[53]
>
> Abraham Maslow, psychologist

At its highest level, your Authentic Self is free of fear, of desire, of anger, shame and regret. In their place are peace, compassion and love. This is what is meant by summoning your better nature. Your better nature has always been present, emerging occasionally. So why not put it front and centre of everything you do?

Of course, you cannot remove every trace of you Conditioned Self. Indeed, there is no need to. You have many useful learned behaviours such as reading, writing and how to be a functioning human being. You possess many traits and attitudes that are worth keeping. It is not a straightforward shift from your Conditioned to Authentic Self, and it helps if you ask yourself if this aspect of your conditioning is serving you or not. Be discriminating, honest and decisive as you declutter the attic of your mind, and choose what to keep and what to discard.

a discerning eye for significance

Working out what you want sounds simple, yet it can take many years to figure out, especially if the different parts of you have conflicting answers: part of you wants to be successful, part of you happy; part of you safe and part of you take risks; part of you in control and part of you dependent. Often, you may think you know what you want, but have not thought it through properly. Or you are following a trajectory based on your perception of what you think your parents, friends and family want.

In *Groundhog Day*, Phil can experiment with the different parts of himself. He can see how living safely compares to living riskily, or how taking advantage of others compares to caring for them. We have less scope than him, so we need to find our own way of determining how we should live. We need to get in touch with ourselves and integrate our thoughts, feelings and values, so we become clearer about what we want and what really makes us tick. This calls for discernment. If you want to be clearer about how to lead your life, you have to be more discerning, which means reflecting long and hard about what you want without distraction. It involves stripping away the trivial and identifying what is most significant to you.

Phil becomes more discerning through continuous trial and error. He is able to establish what he most wants by previewing multiple life strategies and realising that he is more than his situation, his habits or his personality. This approach will help you too. You are not your job, nor your marital or parental status. You are not your income or house value. You are not your height, your weight, your body type or your age. You will realise that you are so much more than any of these, when you discern who you are beyond them.

Over countless repetitive days, Phil discerns the difference between satisfying his ego and fulfilling his genuine needs. Like millions of us, he has to differentiate between means and ends. He initially wants wealth and fame because he believes these are the means to achieving the end he desires – a sense of love, meaning and contentment. In the end, Phil finds the direct path to this end. He discovers that he can bypass all the trivial distractions of minor celebrity, and find the love and peace of mind that he really wants by being authentic. By giving up the means, he gets to the end more rapidly and more securely.

Phil has to find delight in the 'doing' of his immediate activities, because there is no future for which to prepare. He has to find happiness in the now, because 'now' is all he has. In the process, he learns to distinguish the miracle of everyday life from the illusory aspirations of his Conditioned Self.

You can learn a great deal by paying attention to Phil. Indirectly, he is acting on our behalf. We want to see him do more and more crazy things. He is like the mischievous boy at school whom the other children goad to play the pranks they are too afraid to do themselves. In many ways, he enacts our own fantasies.

Have you ever wanted to know the future, so that you could use it to influence people and events? Have you ever imagined a life of unadulterated pleasure doing whatever you want with no consequences? Such desires are entirely natural, and part of what is often known as our 'shadow self'. The eminent psychologist Carl Jung believed that we all have a shadow self that reveals our deeper emotions and intentions. In our everyday lives, we learn for the most part to control these thoughts through self-discipline. Phil's actions allow us to witness what happens when our shadow self runs the show.[54]

He eats and drinks and has sex as much as he wants. He is living the life you might have dreamed of, or might even have led at one time. He can satisfy every appetite, indulge every whim. He symbolises the fantasy of our consumer culture: you can have whatever you want whenever you want. But this fantasy is a delusion – and like King Midas's it turns into a nightmare.

When you are discerning you can recognise your fantasies for what they are. You are able to consider the implications of what you think you want, and anticipate the longer-term impact. You are able to rise above your need to control, to be perfect, to be approved of, to seem powerful or to stay secure. You listen to a deeper inner voice that will help you recognise what is right. As you are still and listen intently, you hear your own voice, and not that of your disapproving parent, competitive friend, demanding spouse or materialistic culture. This is the voice of your Authentic Self.

which path will you take?

One of the hardest challenges we face is deciding which path we want to take in life. Phil was faced with choosing between the paths laid down by his Conditioned Self and his Authentic Self. Straddling both is hard, leading to ambiguity and dissatisfaction. I know this because I tried and failed. My experience of living in California for five years really brought this home.

At the heart of my dilemma was a conflict between my values and my lifestyle, as mentioned earlier. I wanted to be an environmentalist and a green entrepreneur, but had a massive carbon footprint, taking flights to and fro, from London to LA. I talked about voluntary simplicity, but lived in an 8500-square-foot home in Rancho Santa Fe, one of the wealthiest communities in the USA. It never felt right, but I did it anyway, as I was still being directed by my Conditioned Self.

I underestimated the power of my conditioning, and how tied up my self-esteem was with my material status. I knew this was wrong, and I wanted to change, but I was seduced yet again by the illusion that I had to project a successful image. My values and lifestyle were misaligned, and I distracted myself to avoid the truth. I was playing out a life I did not endorse through force of habit, as a result of which I was neither comfortable in the environmental movement nor as a member of an affluent Californian community. I had split myself into two contrasting parts, and failed to integrate my values and behaviour in the way that Phil had managed by the end of the film. I wanted personal transformation, but only on my own terms.

Despite my best efforts, I was still primarily a consumer, rather than a contributor. I was depleting the earth's resources at an alarming rate. My footprint was many times what is sustainable: my house was too big; I owned too many things and I travelled too much. Then, recession hit. I went through a divorce. My finances dwindled rapidly and I no longer was able to afford my previous lifestyle. As I had been a consumer first and foremost, my identity started to disintegrate before my eyes and it was painful.

It was a disturbing experience for my material, Conditioned Self, but ultimately liberating for my Authentic Self, to which it all made perfect sense! It was growth not failure. It was the most important lesson of my life. I realised that an authentic life does not need everything to turn out right. I learned that I had to build on what I had today, not what

I wanted tomorrow. And it helped me to move towards the best version of myself.

> The achievement of your happiness is the only moral purpose of your life, and that happiness – not pain or mindless self-indulgence – is the proof of your moral integrity, since it is the proof and the result of your loyalty to the achievement of your values.[55]
>
> Ayn Rand, novelist and philosopher

accepting the truth about you

Engaging with yourself is hard. It means accepting the truth about who you are and why you do what you do. Such a fierce honesty can be unsettling as you have to face your shadow self and feel vulnerable.

Phil has to accept that he is making himself unhappy, and that he needs a new personal story. If you want to change your life, you probably need to change your story too. If yours is a negative personal story, that means you look for explanations for how you feel, and tend to search for negatives to explain your failures, making you feel worse. Your gloomy outlook is reinforced by negative interpretations of events, leaving you to dwell on perceived failings, when a brighter outlook would have helped you see a better result.

The problem is that you instinctively look outside of yourself for reasons to explain how you feel. This is what Phil does.

He blames the town, its people and the time loop. But there is another dimension to this for him. The time loop is a mirror that forces him to eliminate every trace of self-deception with its unforgiving reflection. He cannot run fast enough to stay ahead of the creeping realisation that his personal story is profoundly flawed. Only when he switches from resisting to accepting the truth is he able to move on.

Phil has to confront his anxieties and acknowledge his power-lessness. This is liberating in subtle ways. In exchange for less choice, he becomes less confused and more able to discern a way forward based on accepting his predicament. His person-ality and world view are exposed as flawed and unsustainable, as the structure of his previous fast-paced media lifestyle collapses to reveal his character deficiencies. Phil witnesses himself being stripped of status and supports, having pushed his Conditioned Self as far as it can go until, like a balloon, it bursts. By first reaching and then surpassing the limits of his old life, he lays the foundations for a new one.

According to Buddhist thought, it is only when we cannot stand the never-ending cycle of misery anymore that we awaken. As Phil awakens, he accepts what he can and cannot change. He can alter his Conditioned Self, but he cannot alter reality. When you accept what you cannot change, you free up your energy and abilities to focus on what you can change.

The act of accepting yourself, your past, other people and the world is extraordinarily powerful. Indeed, it is the first step for many effective change programmes such as Alcoholics Anonymous and Acceptance and Commitment Therapy.[56]

> **God grant me the serenity to accept the things I cannot change; the courage to change the things I can; and the wisdom to know the difference.**
> 'The Serenity Prayer' from Alcoholics Anonymous

Acknowledging that you are in trouble, and that it might be your responsibility, is difficult. Nobody likes to accept that they might have to give up something they value. You don't like to accept facts that conflict with your cherished beliefs. Questioning and confronting your identity is often distressing.

We all know people who have persevered for years in unhappy, hopeless relationships. They cling desperately to the possibility that their partner will change, when all the evidence shows they won't. It is hard for them to accept that they have made a mistake, and that nothing will improve until they face the truth and walk away. The problem is that they would rather stay stuck in their safe routine than face facts. They prefer to thrash around, trying harder and harder to persuade their partner to be the person they want and need, than to have to challenge their own attitudes and behaviours.

If you are in conflict with yourself, you risk being frustrated and unhappy. If you spend your days wishing the past was different or that people would conform to your expectations, you are setting yourself up for permanent disappointment. I know of many people who spend their lives fighting reality.

They create a story about how unlucky they have been, seeing themselves as victims. They are always searching for something or hoping that luck will start running their way.

Like most of us, Phil only changes when he has no other alternative. Although we always have the ability to change, we rarely demonstrate it until we are forced to – when we reach a point of no return, where the pain of continuing as we are outweighs the pain of changing – and then we are surprisingly adaptive and creative.

We don't like to think too much about problems, about illness, about death. We prefer to fight reality, even though we know we can never win. But the longer we delay acceptance, the harder it becomes.

Acceptance is also triggered by a sense of urgency, like being faced with a life-threatening illness. In fact, research suggests that people who face adversity are often happier and more fulfilled.[57]

Accepting that change is hard is important, as is accepting that the struggle itself is the key to success. Sometimes we have to accept the predicament we are in, and make the necessary changes; other times we just have to accept that we don't have the answers. I accept that I don't know, indeed, can never know all the answers. And when we acknowledge that we don't know, we can also start to clarify what is possible and what is important. It puts the onus on us to find meaning, to create our own values and beliefs.

It is tough to alter our attitudes and pick out what we want to believe in. It often appears easier to adopt another's world view. Yet it can be exhilarating when you break free from your conditioning and choose how you want to live. Ultimately, it is better to accept that you have made serious mistakes and that you are dissatisfied, however painful that is, than to continue to pretend and to live a lie. After all, your life is not a dress rehearsal, and every day you spend in denial is a day lost.

a time for everything

One of the most significant turning points in the film is when Phil accepts that he cannot save an old homeless man. He has to acknowledge the existence of suffering and death, and the fact that he cannot control them. In spite of his great power of foresight, there are limits to his influence. He concedes that there is a time for everything, even death:

> To everything there is a season,
> a time for every purpose under the sun.
> A time to be born and a time to die;
> a time to plant and a time to pluck up that which is
> planted;
> a time to kill and a time to heal . . .
> a time to weep and a time to laugh;
> a time to mourn and a time to dance . . .
> a time to embrace and a time to refrain from
> embracing;

> a time to lose and a time to seek;
> a time to rend and a time to sew;
> a time to keep silent and a time to speak;
> a time to love and a time to hate;
> a time for war and a time for peace.
>
> *Ecclesiastes*, 3:1–8

Phil runs the full gamut of life's ups and downs. He confronts an exacting series of hardships that might seem unnecessary or even cruel at the time, yet are essential to his development. He cannot experience the joy of love until he has experienced the sadness of rejection. He cannot feel hope until he has felt despair. He cannot find his purpose until he has lost his cynicism. When you believe there is a time for everything, you will feel calmer and better able to handle the inevitable fortunes and misfortunes that lie ahead.

In my personal life and career I have experienced many ups and downs, like a game of snakes and ladders, where my fate is determined by the roll of the dice. Interestingly, the game originally illustrated the Hindu notion of Karma, and was reinterpreted by the Victorians to highlight the peaks and valleys we all have to get through, while promoting virtues such as thrift, grace and fulfilment.

Yet there is one valley that few of us want to contemplate, and that is the valley of death. In the West we are obsessed with anti-aging and longevity, terrified of confronting our own mortality. This is unfortunate, because contemplating death reveals the wonder of life. It clarifies who and what is important, and encourages authenticity. People who endure near-death experiences, and sometimes the death of a loved one, often make dramatic changes in their lives.[58]

Phil eventually not only envisages his demise, he welcomes it, and finds new life, despite having tried to kill himself many times. He endures great suffering that clears the way for his enlightenment. Like Phil, you can endure, even embrace suffering, and handle whatever is thrown at you. For, there is a time to engage with your fears and anxieties rather than avoid or deny them. I have had difficulty doing this myself. When dealing with personal dilemmas, I have tended to bury my head in the sand and hope the problems will go away. Of course, they never do. Unresolved, they usually get worse and my anxieties intensify.

So I force myself to engage with whatever is concerning me. I make that difficult decision, complete that laborious task and make that awkward call. Taking action leads to a sense of relief. The task normally proves to be easier than I feared, and the outcome generally better than I expected.

Resolving personal and professional dilemmas are milestones in our development. However unwelcome they appear, you cannot always judge whether given events are good or bad at the time they happen. It helps to be detached and patient. When you acknowledge that there is a time for everything, you will be wiser. You will see the bigger picture, embrace the full spectrum of life's rich experience and better appreciate its mystery.

As you observe your life from a more detached and less emotional perspective, you can expand your awareness so that events and people have less impact on your innate sense of wellbeing. You surrender to the rhythm of life, then you can go with the flow and take pleasure in what others may think is a lousy day.

Sometimes, you know when it is time for change. Phil knows this when he stops getting pleasure from exploiting the townspeople, particularly when Rita gets progressively more angry with him. Stripped of his TV persona and his old lifestyle, Phil becomes desolate. Lost in a world where his skills, earnings and achievements have little or no value, he stares into the abyss. As with many people who lose their jobs or retire, he has to find out who he is without the structure and meaning of his conventional life and career. He has to become more self-aware.

Like Phil, when you become more self-aware, you shed a powerful light on the facade of your Conditioned Self. You begin to notice that your personality and self-image are insubstantial and illusory. You discern how your patterns work and observe your thinking. You see that you are not your patterns; that you created these patterns, and that you can alter them too. You realise that you are so much more than your Conditioned Self, and begin to experience an emerging sense of peace. As you start to reconnect to your Authentic Self, you know that this is the only way to live. At last, you discover who you really are.

SUMMARY

- Beyond your roles and activities is your ever-present Authentic Self, who needs and wants nothing to be complete.

- Engage with your emotions. Once you stop running away from difficult feelings and allow yourself to feel vulnerable you are better able to grow.

- The more you engage with your body, the more relaxed, aware and resilient you will become.

- When you are engaged with your values and live by them, you find greater strength, purpose and meaning in what you do.

- Accept that life is a mystery and that you are imperfect

- To be fully engaged you need to connect each part of yourself, so you are whole.

- Discern what is most significant to you, and the difference between satisfying your ego and fulfilling your authentic needs.

- Accept who you really are, however hard that may be, as it is better to accept that you have got it wrong than to continue deceiving yourself.

- Acknowledge that there is a time for everything. There will be fortune and misfortune, success and failure, good times and bad. Embrace the full spectrum of life's rich experience.

CHAPTER SEVEN

your natural resources

> What lies behind us and what lies before us are tiny
> matters compared to what lies within us.[59]
>
> Henry S. Haskins, writer

As you engage with your Authentic Self, you will discover
that you are more courageous, more resilient and more
resourceful than you ever imagined. You possess your own
natural resources that are always available to inspire, support
and sustain you through life's challenges. In this chapter, you
will learn about these innate talents and strengths that you
may previously have overlooked or neglected. Phil discovers
his own resources during his ordeal in Punxsutawney, and
learns how to apply them in order to survive and, ultimately,
flourish.

Your inner resources might include the following:

- Discernment
- Presence

- Appreciation
- Simplicity
- Grace
- Calm
- Passion
- Authenticity
- Vulnerability
- Courage
- Meaning
- Purpose
- Creativity
- Compassion
- Love

These are the building blocks for a perfect day and a perfect life, and you have them at your disposal whenever you need them.

In addition there are five vital natural resources that Phil discovered, and which we will now look at in detail. They are:

- resilience
- resourcefulness
- agility
- experimentation
- wellbeing

If you develop your innate capacity for these five qualities, you will flourish too.

tap into your natural resilience

One of the most important resources you have is resilience. *Groundhog Day* is a celebration of the tenacity of the human spirit. Phil triumphs against the odds as, every day, he has to bounce back from adversity and setbacks. In the process, he becomes stronger and more resilient. By taking action and learning from his mistakes, he not only survives his ordeal, he is victorious. Nowhere is this clearer than in his relationship with Rita. He bounces back from humiliating rejection and, after countless attempts to be more worthy of her love, he eventually wins her affection.

When you activate your natural resilience, you realise that you are much tougher than you ever thought. When you engage with life head-on, you build character. As you welcome challenges and then overcome them, you grow and evolve. Character is measured by your actions and, as Phil proves, you build it by meeting adversity with courage and resolve.

Being resilient is demanding. It requires great determination. When Phil realises he is trapped, his world literally collapses. His existence becomes groundless. Every comforting aspect of his life dissolves in front of him. Though the days remain the same, there is nothing familiar about his experience. He is forced to make tough choices, completely change direction and, ultimately, reinvent himself. He has to face being alone, with no one who can understand his plight. Not even the local doctor and psychotherapist are of any use. He has to rely on his own resources with no support structure. As it

173

turns out though, his quandary proves to be a blessing in disguise. It is the making of him. He negotiates his way through and broadens his perspective, emerging triumphant.

We all have to deal with great challenges such as illness, failure and loss. At work we have to deal with uncertainty, ambiguity and disruption. The question is how well do you cope and thrive in response to them? The key is not running away from your initial feelings, and instead acknowledging your fears and your vulnerability. Once you face facts squarely, you can decide how you want to respond and then take action. The worst thing to do is to ruminate on what has gone wrong, and the best response is to plan what to do next – and then do it.

You can learn to be more resilient even if you have not experienced big life events like loss, divorce or redundancy. You can always look for an opportunity to learn and grow from setbacks, as they are usually better times in terms of learning life lessons than when everything is going your way.

In the midst of winter, I at last discovered that there was in me an invincible summer.[60]
Albert Camus, author, journalist and philosopher

tap into your natural resourcefulness

A pivotal moment in Phil's transformation occurs after he has taken Rita into his confidence, and told her about being trapped in time. They are in his room talking and as he teaches Rita to flick cards into a hat, she asks him, 'Is this what you do with eternity?' This plants a powerful thought in Phil's mind. Then she suggests that eternity could be a blessing in disguise: 'I don't know, Phil. Maybe it's not a curse. It just depends on how you look at it.' Now he realises that he can change and create a new life. He acknowledges the possibility that his life isn't a pointless hell. Now he has hope, and hope is transformative.

Once Phil starts to see the time loop as a blessing rather than a curse, he discovers his innate resourcefulness. He stops using his resources to amuse himself and manipulate others. Instead, he applies them to enriching his life, as well as the lives of others. He stops wasting his time flicking cards and memorising all the answers on TV quiz shows. Instead, he takes up reading. Reading expands his world and his possibilities. He may never have read a book unless it was assigned, or unless he thought it would help him get rich or attract women. Now he takes pleasure in reading for its own sake.

Excellence in the arts requires a long-term commitment – one that Phil is unlikely to have made before. He might have thought about playing the piano and admired great pianists, but there is little chance he would have found or made the time to learn. By taking a long-term view, his perception of time changes and, more significantly, what he can do with it.

As his skills improve, Phil sets up a positive loop. The better he becomes at the piano and ice sculpting, the more pleasure he finds, and the more dedicated he becomes. His resource-fulness and creativity now take him from a downward spiral of self-pity and isolation to an upward spiral of accomplishment. Absorbed in his new passions, time passes quickly for Phil. It does not matter so much that he is trapped in eternity, because he appreciates the quality of each moment. Artistic pursuits give him structure and purpose, as well as pleasure.

The more Phil spends his time on creative pursuits, the less he spends dwelling on his predicament. He engages with his natural resourcefulness and shapes his future with finesse and inventiveness. Every day he is able to revisit his past and alter his future, going back to every encounter, every incident so he can improve the quality of the day. He becomes an expert at crafting a great life, making the best of the cards he has been dealt. Like a talented artist, Phil fashions a masterpiece from the material of his twenty-four hours.

How resourceful are you? Do you see your life and each day as a blank canvas ready for your artistic input? When you wake up tomorrow, think of the day ahead this way. As you learn to shape your life, you will discover that you have the brushes and paints, as well as the creativity, to make your day a masterpiece.

You may not think you are creative but you are. And this does not mean that you need to be a musician or an artist. It means that you become more resourceful and flexible as you open up to new possibilities.

One day might be very similar to the next. You might not be able to alter the place that you're in or the people around you, but you can change your attitudes, thoughts, emotions and actions. As such, you have more control over your days than you might have thought. So, decide whether today is something you need to endure or if it's an opening to new possibilities – a chance for you to be innovative.

You have infinite potential futures before you; you are only restricted by your imagination. When you broaden your vision, it is like rising above a dense, impenetrable forest and seeing the way out. There is always an exit once you rise above your Conditioned Self and all the stresses and strains you have mistaken for your life. You recognise how the reality that you have created has limited you, and how an open and flexible mindset will enable you to transcend your conditioning and break free of your limits.

Phil does not have a map to guide him, and has to try multiple routes before he can find a way forward. You can draw your own map from closely observing your experience. You can develop your own inner GPS to take you in the direction you want to go. You are far more intuitive and far better at predicting your future than you realise.

There are so many different ways of interpreting and experiencing the world. Take the one that is right for you today, not the one that was right for you as a child. Choose to do the right thing, rather than the easy thing. Creativity is one of your most valuable natural resources. Your ability to create new thoughts, new beliefs, and new behaviours is so powerful. It gives you the capability to choose how you want to think and how you want to live.

> It is something to be able to paint a particular picture, or to carve a statue, and so to make a few objects beautiful; but it is far more glorious to carve and paint the very atmosphere and medium through which we look, which morally we can do. To affect the quality of the day, that is the highest of arts.[61]
>
> Henry David Thoreau, writer and philosopher

A resourceful mindset increases your choices. The time loop forces Phil to continually find ingenious strategies to deal with his deepest fears and break free of his conditioning. This is a great education, because what seem to be the worst events of his life lead to the biggest breakthroughs in his growth.

Phil does not learn from books, he does not attend college. Life is his teacher, and he has to struggle with archetypal forces such as fear and fate to make progress. His world, limited in space and time, is his classroom; direct experience his teacher. He learns by doing. You have your own teacher within you too. You just need to observe, reflect and learn from what is happening moment to moment. Become your own coach and mentor. Lead yourself, so you are always learning from your experience.

Resourcefulness is one of the best strategies to get you out of a rut or a low mood. It makes you more flexible and more responsive. I have found that the most successful and the most fulfilled people tend to have the widest range of tools, perspectives, theories and skills to draw on. Top sportspeople have strategies to deal with every challenge while competing – professional golfers, for example, will adapt their game and their shot selection to get the best performance despite harsh conditions. And top entrepreneurs are able to see more opportunities than others. The happiest people I know are those who can dig deep and see the choices available to them, allowing them to adapt to any situation and meet any challenge.

They, like Phil, are also able to reinvent themselves. You can make the best of your day too and not let circumstances defeat you. You can capitalise on the resources you already have. So why not try something different today? Talk to someone new, walk a different route home or even take up a new hobby. Above all, create a great day for yourself and the people you care about.

tap into your natural agility

When you are limited by the Groundhog Day Condition, you tend to freeze your life into predictable patterns of thinking and behaviour. You lose your spontaneity and vitality as you settle for routine. The challenge is that you are fighting a losing battle – because life is an incessant process of transformation. However strongly you want to maintain the status quo, change continues its inexorable march forward, sometimes quietly, and sometimes with a loud bang. It is inevitable. The question is whether you want to fight it or embrace it.

The relentless, intense pace of change driven by technology, competition, outsourcing, social media, customer expectations and global forces way beyond our control is overwhelming. Like Phil, we must adjust or wither. Flexibility and agility are the optimal attributes for flourishing during these uncertain times. Employers are looking for quick-thinking workers, with the potential to learn and adapt, reinventing themselves swiftly and effortlessly.

I know this from my professional work with hundreds of private and public organisations around the world. As the workplace changes rapidly, there is a huge demand for people who can change with it. A 'high potential' is worth more than what you have achieved in the past, as what made you successful up to now may not lead to success in the future.[62]

Agility is relevant to life outside work too. In our relationships, our communities and in our advancing age we are faced with ceaseless change. You can stay closed, operating in autopilot mode, or be open to a world of possibilities. You can choose whether you want to be a passive victim or a willing participant in the process. You are going to have to deal with wave after wave of disruptive change whatever happens, so why not learn how to surf them skilfully rather than crash into them and drown?

When you are so busy in your outer life, you are often unaware of the impact of your resistance to change. Phil recognises this dilemma precisely because he has the time to look inwards and see his recurring patterns. He starts to challenge them and eventually becomes so self-aware that he is able to replace habit and repetition with continuous inventiveness.

Each night, when I go to sleep, I die. And the next morning, when I wake up, I am reborn.[63]

Mahatma Gandhi,
Indian independence movement leader

Groundhog Day is a story of improvisation and renewal. Phil learns to renew himself every day and see the potential in every moment to move beyond his Conditioned Self. He may be trapped in time, but he can still create an infinite number of potential futures though the power of choice. By reinventing himself he also reinvents his experience of life, moment to moment. He is aware of the infinite potentialities before him as he can observe each moment of the same recurring day in slow motion, rather than remaining lost in thought and activity as most of us are.

Phil's experience is a unique lesson in time management at a deep level, and provides new perspectives which can help you transform your life. Phil masters time not as a time traveller, but as a perceptive student of the process of time unfolding. He makes time work for him and so can you, when you experience each moment with a fresh outlook and awaken to the infinite choices at your disposal. Here lies your ultimate power: the power to choose your thoughts, feelings and actions. You achieve a breakthrough when you are open and spontaneous.

You have many capacities and enormous potential. Your ability to renew and recreate yourself each day and even each second is the supreme human capacity. You can improve your life experience wherever you are, and whatever you are doing. You should always retain hope that you can make tomorrow better than today. As Phil discovers in Punxsutawney, you have everything you need today to make either the worst or the best day of your life. Phil creates both days with his own perspective, and reveals his – and our – greatest treasure.

tap into your natural ability to experiment

If you could go back in time, what would you do differently? What would you go back and change? Some people might make a different career choice; others might pluck up the courage to ask out the person they really wanted to be with. Perhaps you would turn down that promotion to have more time with your family? Or maybe you would stick with your guitar practice, write that book or spend more time volunteering.

An important lesson of *Groundhog Day* is that the process counts more than the specific rules of how to live a good life. It is the process of experimentation, day after day, that is so transformative. Phil develops this in response to his predicament, rather than out of conscious choice. He does not have a clear goal or method for his experiments, but stumbles upon an enriching and rewarding way of life through trial and error. By testing, evaluating and modifying his approach and the different decisions he makes, day after day, he begins to build a life full of joy and meaning.

You can also conduct the *Groundhog Day* experiment. You can assess your own life from different temporal perspectives, and gain the same insights as Phil. By learning from your past, previewing your future and living life to the full in the present – like a time traveller within your own mind – you can become expert at and enjoy the opportunity of practising making changes in your life, evaluating what works and what does not.

Start your life-changing experiment by selecting a simple routine activity that you want to change. Say you have a weekly phone call with a difficult person that you dread – next time you make the call, observe your thoughts and feelings. Write them down and then test a new approach on the following call. For example, you might be able to listen more intently or focus on helping the other person, irrespective of their manner. Measure and record the difference in how you feel, and the quality of the outcome. Then you can evaluate whether it was a success or not, and decide on your next steps.

Every time you do this, you can make small adjustments that can result in big improvements to the quality of your life. As you experiment, you may notice that your thoughts are not inevitable, nor are they necessarily accurate or helpful.

You will begin to free yourself from the ties of habitual responses, and learn to develop new ones in their place that serve you better. When Phil does this, he gains perspective and is motivated to try new behaviours too. You do not need to be stuck in time to do the same. You have the same opportunity as Phil, and you can gain the same positive outcome too.

Experimentation gives you the feedback and the proof on how to live. You can make small changes in one area, just alter one variable, such as how you communicate to your partner when you return home, and then measure and evaluate the results. You may even ask yourself powerful 'what-if' questions that challenge your assumptions, and provide hypotheses for testing. Spend a few minutes now answering these questions and consider carefully what you write:

1. What would you do today if this was your only day left?

2. How would you live if you committed to being happy above all else?

3. How would you spend your time if you shifted focus from wanting more to appreciating what you have?

4. What would you do today if you wanted to create your perfect day?

5. What would somebody else, with the same resources, do differently if they had to lead your life?

Test your answers to these questions and observe what happens. Try keeping a diary in which, every evening, you record the results of your daily experiments in working and living. I have been doing this for many years and every time I have a difficult situation that triggers uncomfortable feelings, I write it down, along with how I responded to it. The simple act of writing enhances your learning, and makes it more likely that you will develop effective new knowledge, skills and habits.

Indeed, if you commit to learning through experience every day, you will gain far more useful knowledge than you would from any degree or other course. When you conduct your life like an experiment, and observe your experience like a scientist you will accelerate your personal growth dramatically. Starting today, you can see better into the future, you can preview different scenarios and more accurately predict the consequences of your actions. Instead of wondering what it would be like to have your time over, you can live in a way that will mean you never want to ask that question again.

tap into your natural state of wellbeing

Of all your natural resources, the most important is your innate sense of wellbeing. We tend to lose touch with this sense, and Phil has to find or rediscover his own after years of struggle. Yours is available to you, and is your ultimate resource for overcoming any challenge in life. It is your coach, mentor and wise grandmother rolled into one. It is an intelligence waiting to be released like a genie from a bottle. You are not alone. You have a best friend within you that is the best version of you.

Just as your immune system will help to protect you from illness, your natural sense of wellbeing will help protect you from fear, anxiety and negativity. You have remarkable powers to heal yourself. If you take care of your own emotional immune system, it will take good care of you. Proper care requires that you nurture qualities such as calm, compassion and integrity like Phil does on his voyage of self-discovery.

When you are quiet and mindful, you can reconnect to your intuitive sense of what is right for you. When you move from thinking and doing to simply being, you engage – or re-engage – with your Authentic Self. There is a deep, stable source of wellbeing available at all times – a faint yet clear voice in the stillness. The question is whether you want to listen and act on what you hear.

You can be content, just sitting in an empty room doing nothing. The sooner you learn how to do it, the better, as one day you will be old and frail, and then you won't be able to distract yourself any more. You may not have family or friends to comfort you. You may be alone, but you will still have your inner wisdom and wellbeing. They will always be there for you whatever happens. In the words of my favourite song, 'You will never walk alone'.[61]

You do not have to withdraw from the world or seek retreat on a mountain top to enjoy this state of innate wellbeing. You just have to withdraw from your Conditioned Self. You can find your own sanctuary in a crowded train, queuing in a supermarket or stuck in a traffic jam on the motorway. Peace is not a destination. It resides within you.

When you are dependent on your fluctuating moods and unable to manage them, your sense of wellbeing is temporary and conditional, whereas when you are engaged with your

Authentic Self you are in charge of your thoughts and feelings, regardless of your situation. You are then better able to override passing moods and access your inner strength and innate wellbeing.

Your state of wellbeing is always available when you need it, even in the most testing of situations. I struggle with low moods, especially when I am tired. At about three or four o'clock most afternoons my energy dips, I feel drained and demotivated. This is challenging enough, but in the middle of the night, these moods can be overwhelming.

I remember waking up one night at 2.30 a.m. It was cold and windy outside and, for what seemed like hours, I was tossing and turning. Every concern, worry and resentment joined forces to take me on. It was like a chain reaction as each negative thought triggered a new one. I started thinking about everything that was wrong in my life – every mishap, misunderstanding and setback was magnified. It felt like I was digging myself deeper and deeper into a hole.

I wanted to get up, but was too tired. I thought about reading, but reckoned that would make it harder to get back to sleep. I was anxious about being too tired the next day, and that the whole week would be ruined. I was catastrophising like a pro.

Then I was struck by a simple thought. What if being awake was fine? What if everything was just perfect and I was doing all the damage myself. What if I completely reframed the way I saw my life? It was all going to be OK. It was OK that it was the middle of the night. It was OK that I had problems. And it was OK that I could not get back to sleep.

I looked at my demons unflinchingly and they dissolved into the night. I knew with absolute certainty that I did not need to feel stressed or worried any more. By shifting my attention away from my fears and towards what was good in my life, I accessed my innate sense of wellbeing. I activated my ability to make every day, and even the middle of the night, a positive experience.

You too have a choice every moment of each day. Do you want to spend your days regretting what you have lost, ruminating on what you do not have and anticipating what you might – or might not – have in the future? Or do you want to appreciate the many wonderful gifts you already have? The choice, as always, is yours.

It's like listening to the radio, tuning in to different stations. You can listen to the station that tells you everything is wrong, or the one that tells you everything is OK. Both stations are always broadcasting, but you are deciding what to hear. It is your radio and your hand on the controls. So choose your favourite station, and play the music that uplifts you. When the music changes or there is static, just retune the radio to the right frequency and turn up the volume!

There is always a full spectrum of good and bad things happening. You cannot dwell on all of them, so why not focus on the good things? If you want to stop concentrating on the negatives, then simply focus on two or three positive aspects of your life. It could be that you have a job, that you are going on holiday or simply that you are alive and well. What you come up with is less relevant than the process of actually focusing on what is right in your life, not what is wrong. If you do this throughout the day, you will make yourself happier and also more productive. Keep on asking yourself, 'What is good about this?' and you will be amazed at the results.

a new old you

The more you use your amazing natural resources, the more you will be able to bring about the changes you want. You are re-engaging with your Authentic Self, the forgotten you.

Groundhog Day is a story of rebirth and renaissance. Phil destroys his old self, his ego, before being reborn as a new person. He finds new meaning and identity once his environment collapses. He forges his new identity from choice, not reactivity, and from his values not from his conditioning.

By being immortal, Phil gains a new understanding of his own mortality. He leaves the time loop and returns to normal time, facing the certainty of eventual death with new insights and the resolve to make the best of every day. Once he is mortal again, he knows with all his heart what is most important in his life. Back in 'real time' he is able to appreciate the simple pleasure of life, day by day.

Liberated from the time loop, Phil is also clearer about how he wants to live. Letting go of what he thought he wanted, he finds what he *really* wanted and needed all the time. Punxsutawney, the town he tried to escape from, has everything he ever needed. In the last scene, he even suggests to Rita that they live there, or at least 'rent to start'.

Would you like to experience such a magnificent renaissance – to forge a new identity, and start all over again? For many years, I was dissatisfied with the *old me*, and had a vision of an ideal *new me*. The problem was that I did not truly commit to the new me and, instead, I led a life that was inconsistent with my values. I was stuck in purgatory between espousing my new values and not living congruently by them, as I mentioned earlier. I did not practise what I preached to others, or to myself.

So, how do we transform, realise our full potential and achieve self-actualisation. This is the final stage in our development after our other physical and social needs have been met. It is a coherent set of beliefs and behaviours that help us lead a fulfilling life. A self-actualised person is someone who is psychologically healthy and, according to Maslow, displays these qualities:

- They are 'open to experience'.
- They have an 'accurate perception of reality'.
- They are 'attracted to the unknown'.
- They enjoy a 'freshness of appreciation'.
- They are spontaneous and creative.

- They are accepting and stable under pressure.
- They prefer to focus on problems outside of themselves, rather than be introspective.
- They are autonomous; they feel genuine empathy to other people and the wider world.[65]

This is what it feels like to engage with life and with the real you. This is the extraordinary experience of everyday life. This is your Authentic Self – the very best version of you – and it is available when you access and use your natural resources effectively in everything you do.

SUMMARY

- Activate your own natural resources; you have many of these that you may have overlooked or neglected.

- Your natural resilience enables you to be mentally tough and bounce back from adversity.

- Your natural resourcefulness empowers you to be more creative and give you more choice, so you can make the most of every opportunity and every challenge.

- Your natural agility makes you more adaptable and flexible than you realise. You can embrace and thrive during periods of change, and reinvent yourself when necessary.

- Your natural ability to experiment allows you to test, measure and evaluate different approaches to life, so you can imagine various scenarios and choose to live differently.

- You have a natural state of wellbeing and a powerful intelligence that are always there to guide and nurture you.

- Your natural resources can help you to achieve self-actualisation, enabling you to unlock your full potential and be your Authentic Self.

engaging with the world

> If you want others to be happy, practise compassion; and if you want yourself to be happy, practise compassion.[66]
>
> His Holiness the Dalai Lama and Howard C. Cutler in
> *The Art of Happiness*

Once you have engaged with life and with your Authentic Self, there is one more stage left, and it is the most demanding one. This is engaging with other people: with your family and friends; with your work colleagues; with your community and with the wider world.

One of the reasons I love *Groundhog Day* so much is that I identify with Phil's struggle to engage with other people. I can relate to his sense of entitlement, impatience and selfishness when he arrives in Punxsutawney very well. I know how it feels to be restless, bored and desperate to escape. And I empathise with his withdrawal to the hotel, and his desire to avoid other people. Above all, I share his insecurity.

For insecurity and anxiety have been my constant companions since I was a teenager.

I also know if I want to overcome these feelings, I need to follow Phil's lead. For his transformation is only complete when he transcends his self-absorption, and starts putting other people first. In shifting his focus from what he wants to helping others get what *they* want he finds joy and is finally able to break free from the time loop.

Like Phil, you have a great capacity for love. You may not use it as much as you would like, but it is always there for you. What is more, you do not need to wait to fall in love to experience it. You can be a loving person from this second on. When you speak and act from your Authentic rather than your Conditioned Self, you will feel more loving towards people. They will like and trust you more as they sense your honesty and openness. Once you commit to engaging, you will also want to help others. And just as Phil does, you will move from being an observer to a participant in the world around you, and feel more love and joy than ever before.

beyond the self

When Phil enters the town he seems to be incapable of authentic love for another person. As he tells Rita, he does not love or even like himself. Once he learns to love himself, however, he finds that he is able to love others too. As he discards his conditioning, he liberates his Authentic Self which is the part of him capable of unconditional love. He summons his better nature and is able to build genuine relationships.

At first, Phil is so self-absorbed that he creates a boundary between himself and those around him. He cannot get beyond his self-serving thoughts and actions until he becomes so desperate that his world view collapses. Once there is no point or meaning to his existence, the old Phil fades away.

Sometimes your world has to crumble around you for you to move on. It happens to Phil and it has happened to me. I felt I had lost everything including my identity. I felt crushed, but it all made sense from the more expansive perspective of my Authentic Self. I had to lose everything to find myself. This was one of the most important lessons of my life.

As an only child and a natural loner, I have been prone to self-absorption and even selfishness, as I've said. I have found it hard to love. Moreover, my idea of love was abstract. I wanted to help charities and causes, but cared less for individuals. For many years, I shared Peanuts character Charlie Brown's view: 'I love mankind. It's people I can't stand.'[67]

I consistently sought either approval from others or to control them. My deeper motive was to bolster my low self-esteem. I found it hard to feel genuine empathy, or acknowledge that they had separate needs as I was so wrapped up in my own anxieties and fears. I did not have the skills to stop ruminating until I learned mindfulness, and could interrupt the patterns more skilfully. The liberating nature of this experience is something that Leonard Cohen describes elegantly:

> **When you stop thinking about yourself all the time, a certain sense of repose overtakes you . . . It's like taking a drink of cold water when you are thirsty. Every taste bud on your tongue, every molecule in your body says thank you.**[68]
>
> Leonard Cohen, singer and songwriter

As you gradually transcend self-centredness, you may notice that you engage more effectively with others. This is a virtuous circle: as you put other people first, your fears, insecurities and anxieties begin to subside, and as you act more selflessly, you notice that others start to feel better about themselves and so do you.

Maybe you help people in the hope of getting something in return, or because you feel it is your duty. You act on ethical principles, rather than natural impulses. You ought to give money to this charity as it is the right thing to do, for example. But when you let go of self-interest, you will want to help others for its own sake, not for any anticipated outcome. When you fully engage with another, you stop feeling separate as the boundaries between you and them start to melt away.

The joy of giving is now confirmed by studies. It reduces stress, makes us less angry and boosts our wellbeing.[69] Empathy, compassion and strong relationships are essential to our happiness. You will also learn most about yourself through your interactions with other people. They mirror your strengths and flaws, your defence mechanisms and every subtle quirk of your personality. Interacting with others enables you to understand your behaviours, your values and your habits in action. Sometimes you will see an alignment between how you think you are, and how they see you, but sometimes you will see a marked difference: you might think you are empathic, but others feel you are distant; you may believe you are flexible, but others see you as rigid.

Your family, friends and colleagues are the ultimate test of how far you have changed. At work, 360-degree feedback is increasingly popular, whereby a manager is assessed by their boss, their team, their peers and themselves. Typically, their self-evaluation is at odds with that of their colleagues. But if the manager has the awareness, the honesty and the courage to accept the results and heed the advice, then they can make great progress in their career and their personal development. How do you think you would do at work and at home if you underwent such an assessment?

loving yourself and loving others

When Phil learns to love himself he is better able to love others too, and stumbles upon a whole new emotional landscape to explore, delighting in the intense, sensual nature of his new life. Since his mind is full of love, he has no space for selfish, negative thoughts.

He feels the irresistible urge to assist as many people as possible. He may only have one day, but he can see the ripples spreading from his actions, and the difference between creating positive and negative waves. This is a very different Phil. He is affectionate not distant, optimistic not cynical, humorous not sarcastic and relaxed not tense.

Here is an excellent example of the wisdom of *Groundhog Day*. Phil performs good deeds for their own sake, not for reward or kudos. He does not want or need to be admired as a philanthropist. After all, with no tomorrow, nobody will remember what he does anyway. Whether it is catching the boy falling from the tree or just chatting in the restaurant, he takes pleasure in simple contributions and encounters. He has become a caring citizen serving his small town.

Phil also acts in the right spirit, with enthusiasm, grace and humour. He does not change through good intentions. He changes by engaging with the world and through his relationships with others. It's what we do that counts, not what we intend. You may intend to spend more time with your elderly uncle, but do you? You may intend to help your local community, but what have you actually done? I am guilty of this myself. I watch a documentary that inspires me to live more sustainably, but then I don't bother to turn off my computer at night. I love the big, abstract ideals like saving the planet, but struggle with the small details of saving more energy each day.

Whatever your intention – whether it's reducing global warming, poverty or homelessness – it all comes back to taking personal responsibility. We become more compassionate in our thoughts and our behaviour when we see the results of our actions. Like Phil, we need to understand that there are consequences to our behaviour. When we do this, we can find purpose and by helping others too. When we look beyond our own needs, we appreciate that an ethical life is also a good life, and that selflessness trumps selfishness. When you genuinely want the best for another, something magical happens: you let go of your own worries and find new clarity and inspiration; you let go of the need to please, to impress, to cajole or control and just accept another person as they are.

a labour of unconditional love

Love is demanding. It takes many years for Phil to become a loving person. He can see the benefit of investing in the piano; he cannot imagine any benefit from investing in connecting with others. A long-term relationship seems impossible, as nobody will remember him, or what he says or does, the next day. Love, or even friendship, seems pointless in his 'one-day' lifetime. Where would be the reward for him?

It takes him a very long time to learn that being loving is its own reward. First of all, he has to overcome his yearning for pleasure and instant gratification. All he wants initially is a one-night stand, and he knows that he can get Nancy into bed by the end of the day. For a while, he lives the fantasy of many singles: sex without any responsibility. Yet the fantasy soon loses its allure and Phil realises that he is condemned to a series of sexual encounters devoid of intimacy. He has come up against the boundaries of a life based on selfishness and pleasure seeking and, like other 'entitled' people who generally get what they want, he starts to obsess about the one thing he can't have – Rita.

Phil's relationship with Rita is the lynchpin of the film, and the touchstone for his transformation. At first, he tries to seduce her through ingenuity and deceit. Night after night, he learns every possible detail about her life. He spends his days learning French poetry to impress her. He knows her preferred drink, her favourite toast and her hopes and aspirations. He then uses this knowledge in conversation to try to build a rapport with her. He pretends to have the same interests and values, and every night gets closer to her.

He objectifies her. She is like prey to be hunted, not a woman in her own right. He adapts his own personality to match hers, promoting a false self in the hope of winning her over. He employs the same flirting and seduction techniques that are promoted in many books and magazines. This is about power not intimacy; lust not love.

Phil gets so far with his act, until the moment he tries to get Rita into his bed on their first date. Just when it looks like he will succeed in seducing her, his strategy suddenly stops working. Rita intuitively knows there is something wrong and tells him bluntly, 'I could never love someone like you, Phil, because you'll never love anyone but yourself.' His response to this is very revealing: 'That's not true. I don't even like myself.'

He uses guile to win Rita's affection, because he does not believe she would care for the real Phil. In response, she exposes his insecurity and insincerity. She is the immovable rock that his manipulation and lies cannot shift. She is the benchmark against which he must measure any progress he is capable of. She has always been authentic and loving. She is not pretending or playing games. It is Phil who has to grow up and become deserving of her affection.

Accepting that he cannot win Rita with seduction techniques, Phil starts to pay attention to her as a human being, not merely as the object of his desire. He becomes worthy of her love when he becomes a loving person like her. He stops *pretending* to be the man Rita might fall in love with and starts *being* that man. It is only when he is authentic and abandons his projected image and hidden agenda, that he achieves a genuine breakthrough.

Rita only falls in love with Phil when he is genuinely compassionate and loving. She knows this intuitively, just as she knew earlier that he was a philanderer. By loving people, Phil becomes lovable. Even at the end, when Rita wants to spend time with him, he puts the needs of others first. He tells her, 'Can I have a rain check? I've got some errands I've got to run.' He is not acting to impress Rita. She does not even see his 'errands' as he saves the boy and the official, and helps the old ladies with their car. Knowing that they will have accidents at specific times, he places their needs above what he wants to do – that is spend time with Rita. This is genuine altruism.

This is a significant leap forward. Phil realises that Rita loves him for who he is – not for his power to manipulate time or because he is a TV weatherman. He does not need to impress her any more. He just needs to be his Authentic Self, for this is the man that Rita loves.

Think about the relationships in your life. How much of the time are you seeking to impress, or play a role to achieve an effect? In the end, like Phil, we all discover that a successful relationship has to be built on honesty. Moreover, you cannot look to the other person to fix your problems, or complete you. Nobody can save you or make you a happy person. And you cannot look to your significant other to give you significance. Only you can save yourself and gain the significance you want. You have to complete your own development and become fully authentic. And once you are strong, secure and independent in yourself you can you enjoy a strong, loving relationship.

Love is the free exercise of choice. Two people love each other only when they are quite capable of living without each other but choose to live with each other.[70]

M. Scott Peck, psychiatrist and author

Phil has to engage with his Authentic Self to engage with Rita. It takes him years to reach this point, and it is the same for all of us. There is no short cut to unconditional love. It is all or nothing. Unconditional love has no terms or expectations. You love what is. It is a lasting feeling that does not attach itself to a person or object. It is present when you are on your own, or whether you are with your lover, child, friend, neighbour, colleague or stranger.

Unconditional love is an irresistible force that lifts you above your Conditioned Self, and connects you to other people and the world at large. As this happens, you find purpose and meaning in everything you do. You are in a state of grace, where every day feels like that wonderful day when you fell in love for the first time.

Dependent love, on the other hand – where you become so dependent on the other person to feel good about yourself that you feel intense pain when they do not conform to your expectations or your neediness – destroys grace. If they are late or they do not answer your call, you begin to speculate where they are or who they are with; if they do not give you constant approval, you feel unloved; if they do not take you everywhere they go, you feel abandoned.

I know all too well that such pain is not caused by love. No, it is the result of anxieties, fears and insecurities. Love should not hurt so much. Authentic love feels natural, wonderful and joyous. It blossoms when you want a relationship to enhance your life, not when you need one to fill the void within you.

It has taken me a lifetime to appreciate this wisdom. I have been needy. I desperately wanted someone else to save me and to restore my self-worth. Yet nobody could ever do this. Only I could satisfy my needs, still unfulfilled from childhood. Only I could fill the gaping hole within. And only when I had overcome my fears and begun to love myself first, could I be whole. After many years of searching and some therapy too, I have learned that you can only experience genuine, lasting love when you are fully engaged with life and yourself. You need to be self-aware before you can be genuinely aware of others.

When Phil becomes a loving person, he loves his life too. He loves Rita, he loves himself and he is loved by Rita. And her love is the key for him to open the door to tomorrow. Now he has proved himself to be loving and compassionate, he is released from the time trap and moves forward to the next day, 3 February. Phil has fully embraced the present moment, other people and the world around him. He has completed the last stage in the journey to a perfect day.

a new love of life

We all have a huge capacity for unconditional love and unconditional joy. We make the decisive breakthrough when we commit to love. You might feel that love is confined to romance or family, yet there is a love greater than this. It is love you feel for yourself, for life, for other people and the world. It is the sensation of awakening and experiencing overflowing joy. Above all, it is a feeling, not a thought or a concept.

Major personal change is usually accompanied by catharsis. It is not a controlled quick fix. When you let go of your Conditioned Self there is a tremendous release of old emotions. This often happens in therapy or during times of enormous stress.

Buddhists believe that once we are in touch with our own suffering, and become aware of the nature of suffering, we instinctively want to alleviate the suffering of others. In the Parable of the Mustard Seed, Buddha teaches us how to accept suffering:

A woman has lost her only son and is inconsolable. She cannot accept his death, and carries his body to her neighbours asking each one for medicine as though he were still alive. Eventually, she meets the Buddha and asks for his help too. He asks her to gather mustard seeds from homes that have not been touched by death, and bring them back to him. Every house she visits has been touched by death, so she is unable to collect any seeds. When she returns empty-handed to the Buddha, she realises the universality of death and suffering. Now she is able to bury her son and accept his death.

Acceptance is transformative. If you have ever witnessed suffering first-hand, such as being with a dying parent or friend, you'll know that it changes you. At the moment, I am coming to terms with my mother's suffering. At nearly ninety-two years old she is struggling with many ailments including deafness and early dementia, and a few months ago we moved her to a care home. Watching her in bed coiled up like a frightened toddler is heartbreaking. She is confused and disorientated, slipping in and out of lucidity. As her only child, I do what I can, but I find it unbearable to see her in this state.

When I visit her, my first reaction is to leave as I find it so hard to cope with her plight. But I force myself to sit with her and hold her hand. I look into her eyes and feel love and compassion, albeit mixed with pain and anxiety. By confronting my fears and sense of loss, I am able to stay with these difficult feelings and find new strength. Of course, I wish she were healthier, but I can do nothing to change that. Feelings of denial or regret just get in the way of our relationship. We may not talk, but we are united. She knows I love her and I know she loves me without any words being spoken.

Spending time in the care home and witnessing a succession of infirm, vulnerable, elderly men and women has opened my eyes to the terrible challenges of ageing. I could never have reached this point from watching a documentary or reading research about dementia. I had to be in the thick of things and gain direct experience.

love is everything

The time spent with my mum has further revealed to me that the most valuable lessons come from being authentic in our ordinary interactions with family and friends. Acknowledging the frailties of a parent, sharing our fears with a friend or admitting our weaknesses to our spouse are the building blocks for genuine growth. I feel that I have been spending my life trying to be extraordinary while missing out on the ordinary magic of everyday life. By facing up to my fears and allowing painful feelings to play out, I have noticed a subtle change. I have realised how ordinary I am.

Since childhood I have tried to be different, to stand out from the crowd. Being six foot five has helped, but more important to me has always been to appear superior. Until recently, I applied this to good deeds too, so I could feel morally superior. But this is not authentic compassion. My so-called good deeds were merely serving my yearning for approval and achievement. I wanted to help myself, not others.

Sometimes it is easier to be authentic with strangers than with our families. Nowhere is the power of recurrent patterns more damaging than at home. We lock in to patterns of behaviour and responses that block empathy and under-standing. When was the last time you really listened without judgment to your spouse, your partner or your children?

If you feel stuck in a particular relationship, it might be because you are caught in a dysfunctional pattern of commu-nication or non-communication. Try communicating with compassion. Look into the eyes of your spouse or child and consider how they would want you to make them feel. Then you stop focusing on what you want, and give them what they want. Soon you grasp that the two are the same.

Look around you. Who in your family or among your friends and colleagues needs your attention? Who can you engage with? Who can you communicate with in a way that breaks through old, dysfunctional patterns? Phil ultimately finds meaning through his connection to other people. It is doubtful whether he would have changed so radically if he had been marooned on a desert island for the same period of time.

How connected are you? How much do you know about people at work? How many of your neighbours do you talk to at length? When you meet people, do you assess them straight away in terms of their potential value? Are they attractive, well-dressed, wealthy? And do you think, 'What can they do for me?'

When I lived in California everyone seemed to be after something. Every party and event was an opportunity to network, and to establish new contacts for personal gain. Everyone judged everyone else and friendship was viewed as a means to an end, not an end in itself.

How often have you scanned a crowded room to see who might be useful to you? How often have you been talking to someone while glancing around for someone more valuable to meet? How often have you communicated like a talking CV?

If you have to spend all your energy proving your worth to someone else, exaggerating your qualities and promoting your achievements, you risk building a relationship founded on an illusion: the illusion that you are perfect. You are selling yourself as a product – and you are selling yourself short.

We should stop thinking of meeting new people in terms of how they can contribute to our personal and professional goals, and think more about friendship. How often do you just 'hang out' with people like you used to do at school or college?

Phil has the time to make friends, yet it takes him a long while to get around to it. It is only through the constant repetition of contact that he develops any form of relationship. Imagine if you knew everyone on your street, all the intimate details of their lives, like Phil does. Would you stop stereotyping or judging them, and develop friendships instead?

The wisdom of *Groundhog Day* teaches you to make acquaintance with your neighbours and to be active in your community. When you pay attention, your local streets stop being anonymous thoroughfares on your commute and come alive in new and exciting ways. There are extraordinary people and stories in your midst. There are people on the periphery of your vision waiting to be brought to the centre. When you open your eyes, you open your heart. You realise that your neighbours are just like you, and they are probably feeling just as disconnected as you are. Try listening to them.

Stop thinking about what you need to be doing next, or what else you could be doing now, and simply be present with that person in the moment.

Phil only had twenty-four hours to build relationships before people would forget him. You have the benefit of normal time and people who will remember you. Think for a moment of all the daily interactions you have with people by phone, email or face to face. Now imagine what would happen if you treated each encounter as a chance to improve someone's mood or enhance their day. You don't have to make grand gestures that might seem insincere or pretentious. Just show simple courtesy or recognition. You might soften your tone of voice or offer a welcoming smile, for example.

Engaging with people is demanding. Overcoming shyness and caution, we open our hearts up to others and make ourselves vulnerable. We have all had the experience of trying to make friends and being rebuked or exploited. Sometimes we try to avoid this by restricting our circles to people 'like us'. We feel more secure building our social networks around shared interests, beliefs and education.

The 'new, improved' Phil enjoys meeting people outside his normal circles. He does not spend time with lots of media types, aside from Rita. He meets people from all walks of life and learns to see the value in all of them. Through Phil we can learn to appreciate the pleasure of genuine community, friendship and relaxed conversation. One of the reasons so many of us love Punxsutawney in the movie is that we are nostalgic for the security and familiarity of small-town life, where neighbours all know each other and always make time for a chat. We want to find our own Punxsutawney. We want to come home.

An increasing amount of research demonstrates a strong link between our wellbeing and our relationships, the number of true friends we have being a far stronger contrib utor to our happiness than our possessions.[71] And 'true friends' here does not mean our followers and connections on social media – there is no substitute for the close friends who you see in person regularly.

We yearn for friendship and, above all, we yearn for intimacy. Rita falls in love with Phil when he replaces pretend intimacy with authentic. When he *feels* love, everything changes. He is no longer a spectator in life; he is a participant. People then like him as Phil Connors the man, not Phil the TV personality. Love breaks down the boundaries between Phil and Rita, and also between him and the towns-people.

There is no certainty that you will find the love that Phil does. But what I do believe is that by putting others first, you will greatly increase your chances of doing so. For after Phil has been trapped for thousands of days, after he has tried every possible tool and technique to cope, the only strategy that works is love. He learns what you must inevitably come to know, what your Authentic Self has always known: love is everything.

engaging with the world

> I've learned that people will forget what you said,
> people will forget what you did, but people will never
> forget how you made them feel.[72]
>
> Maya Angelou, American author and poet

Harnessing the wisdom of *Groundhog Day* does not just depend on finding romantic love. As I explained in the earlier section on loving yourself and others (see p. 199), Phil found an even more profound love than the romantic version. He came to feel love and compassion towards humanity. This is what the Greeks called *agape*, in contrast to *eros*, which is the passionate love for another person.

As Phil starts loving, he opens up emotionally. When he helps the old homeless man, he sees him as a fellow human being, not an irritating distraction on his way to the Groundhog ceremony. When he feeds and cares for the man it feels right, and when he cannot save him he is genuinely upset. He cannot hide from pain and suffering any more. He is changing the way he sees other people.

One of my favourite moments in the film is when Phil recites the following lines of poetry to inspire a fellow hotel guest (the same guest he previously ignored and later pushed up against a wall in anger): 'Winter slumbering in the open air wears on his smiling face a dream of spring.'[73]

When I watch this scene I think of the hundreds of hotel

guests and staff I have avoided making eye contact with, or not spoken to in a friendly voice over the years. Always rushing to meals or meetings, I tend to shun all human contact. Yet once in a while I chat with someone in the elevator or at the next table in a restaurant and feel better.

When you connect to the world, you feel more concern for humanity. Psychologist Erik Erikson wrote about universal stages of life and introduced the idea of 'generativity' in middle age, contrasting it to 'stagnation'. Generativity is contributing to your community and leaving a legacy, while stagnation is withdrawal from and failing to contribute to it. Phil endures a mid-life crisis and advances from stagnation to generativity. It is a journey all of us must make to remain fully engaged until our final days.[74]

I regularly withdraw from the world, and it can take a great deal of energy for me to want to engage with others, especially if I am feeling tired or miserable. It is one of the hardest habits to break. I know that engagement is healthier than withdrawal. Yet I have always enjoyed being on my own. Perhaps I learned this from being an only child, and from my parents, who tended to spend their time in solitary activities. We did little together as a family, especially in my teens, and I would play chess alone for hours every day, absorbed in its complex world of strategy and tactics.

I found playing with friends much tougher. Lacking the subtle skills learned from living with siblings, I found sharing or considering the needs of others challenging, to say the least.

Now in my mid-fifties, I still find these behaviours difficult. Being a parent has helped, but I still have to overcome my default mode of control and self-centredness.

From an early age, I wanted recognition and approval more than anything, and most of all from my father. I always knew he loved me, but, like so many men of his generation, he could not say it. Again, I still feel this need much of the time, though I am much better at curbing its excesses. One of the benefits of getting older is that the opinions of others carry far less weight. There is a wonderful sense of relief when you let go of the need for approval.

Perhaps the most important thing I have learned is to accept that my insecurities will probably never go away. Instead, I will manage them more effectively. For *Groundhog Day* is not simply a tale of 'before and after'. Once Phil escapes from the time trap, it's likely that he would have reverted to many of his old ways, but he would also be more adept at managing them – at interrupting his negative thoughts and curbing his damaging behaviours.

Phil, me, you and everyone – we are all works in progress. The wisdom of *Groundhog Day* is that Phil learns new choices, new possibilities and new life strategies so he can better navigate his way through the trials and tribulations of everyday life. And he learns most through his interaction with other people.

I am making many of the changes that Phil does in the film.

I engage with more people, with my community and the world, and do not feel so isolated. And, like Phil, I now know that serving others is far more fulfilling than serving myself. I don't need to spend years in a monastery, or be trained by a guru to realise this.

Phil grows through making a positive contribution to the lives of others. He begins by casting his shadow over Punxsutawney and ends by illuminating the town. He no longer insults people or drives them away with his cynicism. Instead, he inspires them with his good cheer and positive outlook. He boosts their self-esteem and draws them to him like a magnet. He even changes his opinion of the Groundhog Day ritual from derision to admiration. This change of heart is reflected in the opening statements he makes in his tele-cast. He goes from, 'This is one time where television really fails to capture the true excitement of a large squirrel predicting the weather' to 'When Chekhov saw the long winter, he saw a winter bleak and dark and bereft of hope. Yet we know that winter is just another step in the cycle of life. But standing here among the people of Punxsutawney and basking in the warmth of their hearths and hearts, I couldn't imagine a better fate than a long and lustrous winter.'

Engaging with the world is the most testing, and perhaps the most important process of all. The rewards are worth it though. Phil gradually realises that he is part of a community, connected to other people. Each decision he makes sends out a ripple that affects other people in good or bad ways.

He accepts his own limits and also that everyone else is limited. He stops fighting reality and takes a more compassionate, positive attitude towards others as he realises that we are all connected.

> **A human being is a part of the whole, called by us 'Universe', a part limited in time and space. He experiences himself, his thoughts and feelings as something separate from the rest – a kind of optical delusion of his consciousness. The striving to free oneself from this delusion is . . . the way to reach the attainable measure of peace of mind.**[75]
>
> Albert Einstein, physicist

Phil is only released from his suffering when he helps others relieve theirs. Likewise, when we help and connect to others we are also more likely to reduce our own suffering. We are social animals and need connection. We might *want* to control other people, but we *need* to connect to them.

What is the point of being in love and enlightened in our own lives if everything else is falling apart around us? If you are truly aware, loving and living at a higher level of consciousness, you will want to take care of other people and also our planet. So, are you going to leave the world a better place than you found it? Are you a citizen of the earth or a consumer of it? If you have children and grandchildren, what legacy are you leaving them?

engaging with your community

Phil has found his place in the world. He has been rootless, and has now found roots in Punxsutawney. He becomes acquainted with the staff and the customers of the local restaurant. He discovers that Doris, the waitress, dreams of going to Paris before she dies, and that Bill, a waiter for three years, likes the town, paints toy soldiers and is gay. As he gets to know the locals he finds that, contrary to the popular saying, familiarity breeds affection, not contempt.

Now, he wants to make a positive contribution. As a weatherman Phil could not see the fruit of his labours. In Punxsutawney he sees the results of his good deeds as he helps many local people in trouble. In the TV studio he was disengaged from his audience; in his new work he engages directly with his community. He does not need fame or a high salary. The work itself is reward enough.

Altruistic behaviour releases endorphins, boosting our well-being and that of the people we are helping. There is even evidence that volunteering reduces stress and can increase longevity. Doing good is feeling good. This is a powerful equation.

In everyday life, who influences you more? Are you motivated more by altruism or self-interest? Do you think about helping others get what they want or helping yourself get what you want?

This has been a major battle in my life. Even as I write this chapter I am thinking about the conflicts I feel every day. I worry about the gap between my espoused values and the life I lead. I am better than I used to be, but there is still some way to go. Some mornings I wake up wanting to dedicate my life to a great cause; on others I want to protect what I have and withdraw from the world. What helps me is to remain self-aware and catch myself before I slip back into the familiar pattern of thinking, 'How does this affect me?'

The best response is to take small, incremental steps in everyday life. You do not have to volunteer in Africa. You can start in your own community, your own office and your own home. What can you do today to help just one person? How can you adjust your behaviour to be more open, more empathic and more compassionate? Subtle shifts in direction and small changes in behaviour accumulate over time, and turn your ideals into reality.

help yourself by helping others

Make a list of good deeds you want to do and then do them. Phone a relative you have not spoken to for years; offer your time to a local group of volunteers; visit the new neighbour on your street. Don't think too hard about it. Just perform these good acts every day for a month and record how you feel. Write the first three you are going to do here:

1

2

3

Remember how much Phil achieves in a day when he redirects his energy from serving himself to serving others. This is the extraordinary power of love combined with purpose in action. Just observe the full spectrum of his responses to the insurance salesman, Ned Ryerson, for example. Starting with denial, Phil moves through avoidance, contempt, anger, violence, overfamiliarity, and – finally – genuine friendliness.

Phil only had the people of Punxsutawney to engage with. You have the world. Start small and go deeper into the world around you. Then you will see the results of your actions. As you love others, you strengthen your Authentic Self. You shed the worn-out, negative thoughts, beliefs and desires that kept you unhappy. Instead, you are enhancing your physical and emotional wellbeing.

Volunteering is the perfect antidote to the cutthroat competitiveness of modern life. Whatever you decide on, do it in the right spirit and without expectation. It does not matter what other people do or don't do, or what they say or don't say. Everyone is at a different stage in their lives.

But you do not have to join a charity to practise compassion. You can help your family, friends and colleagues with good deeds. You can help others by performing acts of kindness, and it will help you too.[76]

You can also be compassionate without taking direct action. You can say silently to everyone you encounter or see during the day, 'I wish you well' or even, 'I send you love'. This might be colleagues or strangers in a crowd. It doesn't matter. What counts is the practice. Every time you wish people well you are boosting your empathy and compassion. You are shifting emphasis from how *you* are feeling to how others are. It may seem strange at first, but it definitely works. I practise this regularly and I notice an immediate improvement in my mood.

Engaging with other people and the world in general is a continuous, dynamic process. It is a journey of a lifetime. Every day, commit to staying engaged in everything that you do. Then you will be able to transcend your Conditioned Self. One of the best ways to stay engaged is to find work that makes a positive contribution to the lives of others. I have found that the happiest people have jobs that give them meaning and fulfilment, and where they engage their values by serving a cause greater than themselves. Phil found genuine happiness through serving others and perhaps this is the greatest wisdom of all.

This does not just mean looking after your family. *Groundhog Day* teaches us to have reverence for ourselves, our neighbours, our town and I believe this extends to everything and everyone. The world needs your help now, and it needs it urgently. Find time to volunteer and help your community. Mentor someone who will benefit from your experience. We are all motivated by different issues and causes; it may be alleviating poverty, curing cancer or supporting a hospice. Choose an activity that you enjoy, that you are good at and that will do you and others good.

For me, the most pressing concern is the environment. I feel we need to engage with our earth, the very source of life. We are part of Nature not separate from it. Yet we are locked into a fast-paced, out-of-control system that is completely unsustainable, and we do not appreciate the beauty or the fragility of our planet. Our wellbeing ultimately depends on that of our ecosystem, which supports life itself. It is only when we slow down and reconnect to Nature that we start to cultivate and feel a deep sense of gratitude and appreciation for the gift of life.

life is indescribably precious

If we are the only intelligent civilisation in the galaxy that makes us indescribably precious and valuable.[77]
Professor Brian Cox, physicist

If you and I agree with Brian Cox that we are the only intelligent civilisation in the known universe, then what does that imply for how we should live during our brief stay on this planet? If we acknowledge how privileged we are and how precious life is, then surely we need to be stewards and take care of our earth?

This is my highest value. I now fly far less than I used to, drive a fuel-efficient car and buy very little. I have shifted my focus to finding a positive way of living that fulfils my authentic needs for meaning, connection and purpose, not my artificial, conditional needs for status, power and recognition.

Groundhog Day is about becoming engaged and falling in love. The same principle applies to us and our world. When we learn to engage with Nature and love our planet, we take responsibility and are accountable for our actions. Living sustainably means being compassionate to all species, and this includes humans. Then we are looking after current and future generations. We are acting as guardians, answerable to our children and grandchildren. This is often called 'intergenerational justice'. For our purposes, it means engaging with our planet.

> **Everyone shares responsibility for the present and future well-being of the human family and the larger living world. The spirit of human solidarity and kinship with all life is strengthened when we live with reverence for the mystery of being, gratitude for the gift of life, and humility regarding the human place in nature.[78]**
>
> The Earth Charter

With determination and imagination, we can satisfy our personal needs, the needs of others, and also our ecological needs. We can change from being selfish consumers, acting out of misguided self-interest to becoming concerned citizens, working for the good of society and the environment.

What is your calling in life? If you are truly aware and engaged; if you love and live at a higher level of conciousness, then how are you going to leave the world in a better place than you found it?

SUMMARY

- A crucial stage in your personal growth is to engage with the world.

- You grow most when you stop focusing on what you want, and start helping others achieve what they want.

- Helping others helps you too. It reduces stress, makes you less angry and boosts your wellbeing.

- There is no short cut to unconditional love.

- Unconditional love is an irresistible force that lifts you above your Conditioned Self, and connects you to other people and the world at large.

- See each encounter today at work, at home or in your community as a chance to improve someone's mood or brighten their day.

- The happiest people have jobs that give them meaning and fulfilment, and where they engage their values by serving a cause greater than themselves.

- Consider how you are going to leave this world a better place than you found it?

practice makes perfect

> . . . if you only had one day to live, what would you
> do with it?
>
> Phil Connors, *Groundhog Day*

The thought of transforming your life may seem over-whelming. On the other hand, when you think about transforming your day, it feels more achievable. This is a key pearl of wisdom from the film. You can transform your life if you focus on one day at a time; by improving the quality of each day, you can change your life. This is how Phil not only survives his predicament, but ultimately masters the art of living. He has to decide how to make the most of the one day that is available to him. You may not be repeating 2 February, but you can create your own ideal day today and every day from now on.

We have looked at how you can engage with life, with yourself and other people, and now there is one more element to complete your transformation. Like Phil, you can create your perfect day with *practice*. Phil may have gained wisdom, but his breakthrough occurred when he turned his new wisdom into consistent action. With continuous practice and experimentation, he was able to develop the habits for building a wonderful life.

Practice is essential if you want to develop new habits, and achieve sustainable improvement in any area of your life. There is always a measurably better way of playing the piano, playing tennis, studying, leading and everything else. And the same principle applies to the art of living – the most important skill of you will ever learn.

When I was at school, all my reports said the same thing: 'Paul tries hard'. I used to think of this as criticism, but now I appreciate that this is my most useful trait. I never stop trying in every area of my life. Yes, I fail a lot of the time, but that's all right. There is a set of life skills that you can learn, practise and master to lead a more fulfilling life, and this includes self-awareness, resilience, resourcefulness and the many others I have covered in previous chapters.

getting better every day in every way

Groundhog Day does not just envision a better way of living, it shows you how you can get there. It demonstrates that each day is a stage in your development, and an opportunity to grow. As the old mantra suggests, 'Every day, in every way, I'm getting better and better.'[79]

Phil measures his progress by the quality of each day, and so can you. When you raise the quality of each day, you raise the quality of your life. This is the promise of making small daily improvements. Phil cannot compare himself to others, as he has done previously, but he can compare different versions of himself as he varies his behaviour from day to day.

So think about today: what did you learn? What worked and didn't work? And what will you do differently tomorrow? When you focus on improving your days in this way, you will realise your extraordinary potential. Surely that is a more inspiring way to think about your time. After all, each day is a gift and a new opportunity to grow, not an ordeal to be endured. However testing your life may be, there are valuable lessons to be learned to help you grow and develop – and there is always hope. As the last line from the film *Gone with the Wind* reminds us, 'Tomorrow is another day'.[80]

To help you with these small daily improvements I recommend that you keep a daily journal to record them, so that they will accumulate and register as significant change. Write down what have you learned every day, what worked and what did not. The more you observe, record, measure and evaluate, the more you will build and strengthen the improvements that you want.

> **Begin at once to live, and count each separate day as a separate life.**
>
> Seneca, Roman philosopher

playing with time

As soon as Phil realises that he is stuck in the time loop, he starts to reflect on the content of his days and discovers he can choose to do whatever he wants. His potential is unlimited because there are no consequences to his actions. He does not need to work, and he has no responsibility. He can do anything he wants in the knowledge that he will wake up the next morning, starting with a clean slate again. Nothing will have changed in the town, and nobody will remember what happened, apart from him.

Phil changes by playing with time. He is inventive and decides to make the best of things, if only to play pranks and have a lot of self-indulgent fun. He gathers information about people and then uses it to manipulate them: he learns Nancy's personal details, and the next day pretends he knows her from school and proceeds to seduce her. Since she does not remember giving him the information the previous day, he can take advantage of her.

Then he learns to use his time more wisely. He creates the ideal day and requires nothing more than what is already present, in the ordinary small town of Punxsutawney on a freezing cold day in February. By experimenting in this way, he becomes more resourceful and creative with his time. Eventually, he is able to construct an ideal day with careful planning. When he is walking in the snow with Rita, she says to him: 'It's the perfect day. You couldn't plan a day like this.' To which Phil replies, 'Well, you can. It just takes an awful lot of work.'

Groundhog Day is a compelling metaphor for those situations where you cannot change what is happening, only your response – whether that's dealing with a traffic jam, a difficult person or a serious illness. Consider what represents your personal *Groundhog Day* right now. Then, when you are resourceful, you are able to change your response and make the best of whatever cards have been dealt to you.

decisions, decisions, decisions

The way that *Groundhog Day* reveals the consequences of every decision Phil makes provides a fascinating insight. He can get immediate feedback on each of his choices, as he is the only autonomous decision maker in town. Everything that happens on the next 2 February is a direct result of what he does today. We can witness and assess the intricate process by which he makes his decisions, and what their consequences are, as everything is brought into sharp focus and in slow motion.

Like Phil, you can make decisions that move you forward or back, and that engage or disengage you. And like Phil, if you take the time to observe and assess your own decision making carefully, you can make better choices too.

Let's try an experiment. I want you to investigate the critical moments and decisions during a typical day, and see how you can create both a 'disengaged experience' and an 'engaged experience' of the exact same day through your moment-to-moment choices.

It all starts when you wake up and are faced with an immediate choice. You can be optimistic or pessimistic; you can focus on opportunities or difficulties ahead; you can set out to learn and grow today, or not. Whatever you decide will affect your mood for the rest of the day. You can disengage and go into autopilot mode; or you can engage with the possibilities that today offers. You can create a terrible day, a mundane day, a good day or a great day. It is up to you. The events and encounters that take place may remain the same, but you can still change the way you experience them.

On the train to work, you can choose to be disengaged as you browse the internet on your phone, and listen to music; or you can be engaged as you plan your priorities, and observe the other passengers, lost in their thoughts, while appreciating the passing sights and weather outside.

When you arrive at work, you attend a meeting and negotiate with an argumentative colleague. You may disengage and go through the motions, avoiding eye contact and sticking to a prepared script to reduce stress. Or you may engage with your colleague, and listen to them with empathy and understanding. By being more mindful and sympathetic, you may turn a possible confrontation into a learning opportunity. The meeting is the same. You have made the choice to change by engaging.

The next critical point in your day is late afternoon, when you are faced with a dissatisfied customer. You are tired and would prefer to postpone dealing with them until another day. You want to disengage from the customer and avoid an anticipated dispute. But what might happen if you engage with them instead? You make the call, you listen to their complaints and take steps to solve the problem. By putting the customer first, you are able to forget about your worries and fatigue. You find new energy and resolve their issues. You also lift a weight off your shoulders by not putting off important tasks until tomorrow.

Your final moment of truth is in the evening. Arriving home, you have a decision to make. You can disengage by mindlessly watching TV all evening, while drinking a bottle of wine to forget your troubles. Or you can engage in activities like exercise, hobbies or conversation. Before bed, you can dwell on the day's woes, or you can write five positive things in your journal to remind yourself of the successes. Again, it's up to you. The day remains the same. It's your interpretation and conduct that vary. Just remember that you will not get this time back, so choose with care.

seeing into the future

Every day you enjoy the greatest gift of being human – the power to choose. I am so thankful that I always have choices, and that there is often a better way forward for you and me. You may decide to live a comfortable, safe existence within self-imposed limits or you may decide to break free, take some risks and try something new. Just remember that you have set your own limits. You cannot blame an invisible force that traps you in time, nor can you blame your circumstances or conditioning. There is almost always a way to use your time more wisely, and make better decisions.

You can also find ways to handle the challenges that you face more effectively. You do not need to possess a unique talent nor be more intelligent or educated. You simply need to be resourceful and find a superior strategy. You can seek out people who have overcome the same challenges as you, and you can model what they do. You have within you the capacity to emulate others. You can alter your beliefs, your thoughts and your actions. I often imagine that there is a 'better version' of all of us that is always present, waiting to emerge. Just like Phil, this 'better you' appears as you engage with your Authentic Self.

One idea that may help you is the practice of previewing your future. In the film, Phil can preview his future accurately as he knows every intricate detail of the town and its inhabitants. He can act in alternative ways and reflect on the impact of each one. He can envisage what would happen if he changes his behaviour towards Rita, and then either maintain or modify the behaviour the next day based on the result. As Rita will be exactly the same the next day, as *it is* the same day, he is able to replicate the results and make his mind up.

Phil can preview various scenarios. He is able to visualise what it would be like to treat a person in another way, to try a new activity or find an innovative solution to a recurring problem. He gets a taster of different experiences as he replays the same day.

Indeed, one of the most effective ways to increase your happiness through better decisions is to preview the impact of the different options you have.[81] So, before you sit down with your manager, for example, you could preview four or five outcomes dependent on different approaches you can take to the meeting. Visualising future scenarios in this way, or writing them down, can help you determine the path you want to take. When you acknowledge that you have more than one way of doing things and take the time to identify and evaluate choices, you can break the habit of making decisions on autopilot or on impulse. Then you can allow your Authentic Self to be heard and not rely on the pre-programmed responses of your Conditioned Self. Put simply, you think before you act.

if i had my time over again

If you want to learn how to make time work for you, you can start by asking yourself a searching question: 'What would I do if I had my time over again?'

To help find the answer, I want to turn to another film. It is called *About Time*, and features a family in which the men are able to travel in time. Tim, the latest recipient of this magical gift, delivers this inspiring message.

> And in the end I think I've learned the final lesson
> from my travels in time; and I've even gone one step
> further than my father did: the truth is I now don't
> travel back at all, not even for the day, I just try to
> live every day as if I've deliberately come back to this
> one day, to enjoy it, as if it was the full final day of
> my extraordinary, ordinary life.[82]

Tim's father had previously advised his son to live each day
twice, which he called 'his secret formula for happiness'. The
first time, live it like everyone else 'with all the tensions and
worries that stop us noticing how sweet the world can be,
but the second time noticing'.

We cannot live the same day again. What we can do, however,
is act as though we have travelled back in time to make the
most of these irreplaceable twenty-four hours and enjoy every
second of them.

I love this concept. Think about it for a moment. Imagine
you had been given the opportunity to come back to this
day once more. What would you do differently? How would
you ensure you enjoyed each moment? What would be most
important to you?

I try to approach every day with this attitude. Why wait until
it is the only day you have left, to live life to the full? Why
waste another moment? I want to live every day as though
it was my only day. I want to make it as perfect as I can.

This does not mean I have to eat at a Michelin-starred restaurant or drive a Ferrari. It has nothing to do with my outer life, and everything to do with my inner experience. I want to feel happy and engaged. I want to love and be loved. I want to savour each second and notice each exceptional detail of my unexceptional life.

When you think about how you might spend your last day (or only day, in Phil's case), what does that tell you about your life now? How much of what you are doing today is the same as you would be doing on your perfect day? Maybe it is time to make some changes. Of course, you have to earn a living and make compromises – we all do. Yet there are always areas where you can improve the quality of your daily experience, and these build up over time, moving you ever closer to your perfect day.

This is another example of the wisdom of *Groundhog Day*. If you change the way you experience each day, treating it as your only one, you will see what was previously unseen, do what was previously left undone and savour what was previously ignored.

There is wonder all around you, all the time. I remember a series of bestselling books called *Magic Eye* that were all the rage about twenty years ago.[83] These were books full of optical illusions – pictures that contained hidden images. As you looked at the picture a 3D image would begin to appear like magic. Every time you looked at it again, you would see something new.

The same is true for our everyday lives. Hidden magic is waiting to be revealed if you just take the time to look closely. Each day is miraculous when you frame your life as a day-to-day journey of discovery. I have found no better way to live than celebrating the unfamiliar beauty of the familiar. You do not need to be a time traveller to enhance your experience of time. You simply need to ask this question throughout the day: am I engaging with life to the full?

Now let's experiment further. What if you really could travel in time? What if you could go back to your past, and revisit a decision that you regret? For example, imagine returning to when you were eighteen and studying for a law degree, when really you had wanted to go to art college. Maybe you would never have become a lawyer. Or perhaps you would have married someone different, or taken that job in New Zealand.

There are bound to be some momentous decisions that you wish you could reverse. As you consider your own turning points, when maybe you took the wrong path, what can you learn? In most cases, you will find that regret or remorse are of little value. After all, you cannot alter the past. Instead, focus on why you made your decision and why you believe it was in error.

Of course, you cannot ever know if it was a poor decision or not, as, unlike Phil in the film, you do not know the consequences of the alternative. It may be that being with the person you think you 'should' have married would have been a disaster. Or that 'dream job' in New Zealand would have been disappointing and damaging to your long-term career.

You cannot know the outcome of what might have been. What you can know are the reasons that led you to take a particular path. Here, you can gain wisdom by being honest and clear about what influenced you in the past. Was it fear? Or maybe the need for approval? Or impatience? More importantly, how can you apply the lessons to make better decisions in the future?

Just as Phil used the ever-repeating 2 February to preview his future and become a better decision maker, you can use your own past to do the same.

You can also use the future to help you. If you are facing a tough choice today, what would the future you advise you to do? Just as you can think about what you would have done differently five years ago, imagine you are five years older looking back at today. What would the older you advise the current you to do?

Listening to and cherishing your imagined future self helps to improve the quality of your present. By applying these different perspectives you get a richer, deeper understanding of your current position.

The most famous example of this method is found in Charles Dickens's *A Christmas Carol* in which the main character,

Ebenezer Scrooge, travels in time to his past and future to gain new understanding of his miserable present existence. Only by acknowledging what he has lost in the past and previewing his meaningless future, is he able to comprehend his desperate present predicament. This terrifying realisation leads to profound transformation. By using time to reframe his sense of self, Scrooge is able to transcend his heartlessness, and be happy at last. Like Phil, he discovers that focusing on others rather than himself leads to joy.

Another example of the power of altering your perspective of time is found in Frank Capra's film, *It's a Wonderful Life*.[84] Unlike Scrooge, the protagonist, George Bailey, is a good man. His problem is that his life has reached its lowest ebb. Believing he has lost the savings of his bank's customers he decides to take his own life – that is until Clarence, an angel, stops him and shows him what would have happened if he had never been born at all.

By taking George on a journey through time, Clarence shows George how many people would have suffered if he had never existed. Just like Phil Connors and Scrooge, George Bailey comes to realise that he has a wonderful life by experiencing time differently. It does not matter whether there were magical forces at work or not, the epiphany is just as striking and just as valid. Your quality of life depends on the quality of your perspective.

We could all benefit from our own ghosts of Christmas past and future, and our own guardian angels. But in their absence, ask yourself the questions below. When you answer them, notice how you already make a positive contribution to other people. You may also see your purpose more clearly, and realise the extent of your legacy.

What would the world be like if you had never been born?

Would the world be a better or worse place without you in it?

Whose lives would be different?

George Bailey was neither a President, nor a philanthropic billionaire. His influence was on a small scale, like most of ours. The point was that he mattered to the people in his town, and he mattered most of all to his family and friends. His nemesis, Mr Potter, was the wealthiest man in town, but he had no friends and little positive impact on others. So, who would you rather be – George Bailey or Mr Potter? George chose happiness and Mr Potter chose wealth and power. Where is your focus?

Live as if you were living already for the second time and as if you had acted the first time as wrongly as you are about to act now.[85]
Viktor Frankl, psychiatrist and Holocaust survivor

Over a hundred years ago, the philosopher Friedrich Nietzsche asked us to imagine living the exact same life again and again for eternity – what he called the law of eternal recurrence.[86] This raises a fascinating question. If you knew that you were going to live your life again and again, what would you do differently to make sure it was worth repeating? Your answer has significant implications. If there is something you would change, then why not change it now?

For example, if you lived for ever, would you focus on improving your status or your character? What would be a better strategy for sustaining happiness and fulfilment? You and most other people would probably answer 'character', and you would be spot on. The more challenging and significant question, however, is whether you follow this principle and live by this standard now? How much time do you spend on improving your status, and how much on improving your character?

Phil focuses on building his character by learning from his experience, not hiring a therapist or being inspired from the pulpit. He reaches his own conclusions, and discovers universal truths. He is able to see the consequences of every action he takes more distinctly than the rest of us, and chooses a way of life that makes the best of every day.

putting it all into practice

Phil learns to make the right choices through trial and error. He could never have transformed his life and flourished without continuous, intense practice. This is how he achieves the breakthrough that releases him from the time loop.

As we've seen, practice is essential when it comes to learning to live well as much as anything else. Phil performs a never-ending series of rehearsals until he achieves expertise. He tries something new every day until he gets it right. By making small adjustments each day he becomes a virtuoso in living life to the full.

If you want to master the art of living yourself, you have to practise, as practice does indeed make perfect. Why not try mindfulness, happiness, appreciation and the other strategies I have recommended? The real work begins when you stop reading and start practising. That's when you start to learn from the best teacher of all – direct experience.

Just imagine how your life would be today if you had done all the things you know you should have done, and learned all the skills that you wanted to learn. Now imagine what it can be like in the future if you do these things from now on.

Let's suppose you wanted to be a competent golfer. You might spend two hundred hours learning the game and improving your strokes – but unless you plan to be a professional, how much difference will that make to the overall quality of your life? What if, on the other hand, you spent the same two hundred hours learning to be happier instead? What if, for two hundred successive days, you spent twenty minutes a day completing a gratitude journal, twenty minutes a day meditating and twenty minutes a day laughing at your favourite comedy sketches? Wouldn't that contribute more to your life?

You may well agree. You may already have read other books that gave you this same advice. But do you put it into practice? Do you recognise the damaging effect of reliving each day under the spell of your Conditioned Self? What are you going to do today to remedy this?

Practice is the conscious development of habits that you want rather than ones you have developed unconsciously. Phil changes by practising day after day for many years. He is not just practising the piano; he is practising new thoughts and behaviours. By stepping out of his automated life into the timeless world of Punxsutawney, he finds the time and space to make deliberate choices, not routine responses to the constant demands and pressures we all face in the 'real world'.

He is able to identify and evaluate every one of his habitual behaviours, every sequence of thoughts and every automatic response. Then he rearranges them into more helpful strategies and techniques through practice. You can do this too when you slow down and learn from your direct experience.

Consider the benefits of taking action today. Instead of settling for acquiring more knowledge or affirming knowledge you already have, why not make the changes you want? The tools and skills you require are available. You just have to make them habitual.

Phil learns by doing. He experiments diligently until he creates his ideal life. He finds what he is passionate about and pursues it. After many years of practice, he is able to discern the routines and habits that will sustain him in Punxsutawney. He structures his ever-recurring day around these habits. He does not just think that he would like to play the piano, he puts in the hours every day. He does not just toy with the idea of helping people, he goes out there and helps as many people as he can.

He also practises what he preaches. He learns to live in alignment with his values. What routines and rituals do you want to structure your day around? What habits do you commit to building?

the game of life

In many ways, *Groundhog Day* is like a game that Phil has to learn, practise and eventually master. At first, he does not know the rules or even the outcome of the game. There are no instructions to follow. He has to figure it all out for himself. He never knows what force is keeping him in the time loop, yet over time he begins to understand the rules better. The game lasts twenty-four hours, and every morning at 6 a.m. it resets in exactly the same position as yesterday, as it is yesterday all over again. All that has changed are Phil's knowledge of the game and his skill levels.

His challenge is to develop a strategy using the resources of the game as creatively as possible to navigate his way through each level, and then out of the game altogether. The resources at his disposal are the town, its people, and the same twenty-four hours. He learns to replay difficult events and problems needing a resolution whenever he wants. Knowing he only has twenty-four hours, he becomes adept at condensing everything into his day, and this intense cramming teaches him how to get the most out of life

Phil has to overcome many obstacles; he is thwarted by detours, false starts and dead ends along the way. Most of his tactics fail, and it takes him thousands of days of repetition to make any progress. Even when he thinks he is making progress, he is not. For countless days he thinks he is winning Rita's affections when, in fact, he is losing her.

Phil masters the game when he solves the puzzle of how to live his day in a peak state. You can see that he appears and sounds different, and enjoys a state of heightened awareness. He looks much happier, and his physical appearance and his voice have changed. He is relaxed and comfortable with himself, and with other people. He has replaced disdain with empathy, and bitterness with cordiality. You can sense his overflowing joy during that last magical day in Punxsutawney. He has a spring in his step, his body language is open, expressing his joie de vivre. Life is no longer a struggle. It is a glorious dance.

When you let go of your Conditioned Self, you win the game of life too. You progress to the peak state that is the reward for being your Authentic Self. You reconnect to the joy, vibrancy and zest for life you might have had as a child. As the weight of anxieties, fears and conforming are lifted, you engage with your natural state of wellbeing that was obscured and dampened by so many years of conditioning.

the definitive course in time management

Through managing his time superbly, Phil is able to squeeze every drop out of his day. He is incredibly productive by the end of the film, achieving a remarkable amount in twenty four hours through careful planning and organisation. In many respects, *Groundhog Day* is, as such, the definitive course in time management.

He shows what you can achieve in one day if you set your mind to it. He masters the quality of his time as well as the quantity of his time and he spends it wisely. He becomes an ordinary superhero whom you and I can emulate. When you learn to master time management in the way Phil does, you will learn a far more valuable skill than how to use schedules, calendars or to-do lists. You will learn how to manage the time of your life, how to make the most of the hours, minutes and seconds you are alive on this earth. Because the one thing you cannot replace or get back is time.

A simple practice that might help you make the most of your days is to focus on improving the quality of each minute: live the next minute as though you have perfected it over years of practice, or as if you were living it the second time around. Then repeat this for one more minute and then another and another. This is how you change, one minute at a time. This is how you create quality time. Higher-quality minutes turn into higher-quality hours, and higher-quality hours turn into higher-quality days.

Phil discovers his power to create quality time as he gradually alters his relationship with time completely: at first, he fights against it; then he tries to manipulate it; next, he tries to survive it; then, losing all hope, he tries to end it. As he awakens, he learns to be present in time. Then he learns to appreciate it, and eventually, he learns to love time, and uses it to help himself and others flourish. Like an alchemist, he has transformed his time into a perfect day and a perfect life.

You have the ability to emulate Phil in normal time. You can move skilfully between present, past and future thinking. You can become better at making time work for you. In the tradition of innovative science fiction, the film alters your perspective by magnifying, modifying and distorting your perception so you can see the world with fresh eyes. Its distinctive take on time travel provides insight into how we can accelerate our development, by decelerating the pace of life. As time stands still, you can watch life go by in slow motion. You can experiment with alternative choices and see their outcomes. Each day becomes a rehearsal for a progressively better way to live. All you need is to learn how to make the best of your time, just like Phil.

daily rituals

Phil's final, perfect day is the culmination of thousands of days of practice. He has had to create his own routines from scratch, so he can make the most of his day. Over the course of time, he deliberately builds a structure to his day on the foundation of simple routines and rituals, rather than the unconscious habits and conditioned response most of us live by. He lives each second attentively and purposefully, not on autopilot.

We are all hard-wired to be creatures of habit, and at heart, you will always be this way. You will always need regular practices and procedures to be effective. But you can make the repetitive nature of your existence work in your favour, by developing rituals that serve you. I have my own daily rituals for a happy life. They include two or three walks, listening to classical music, reading uplifting books and writing for at least thirty minutes. I also practise daily mediation and say thank you many times to affirm my appreciation.

Why not prepare your own schedule of small, regular practices that help organise the life you want to lead? What might you do as soon as you wake up? How might you plan your day? How are you going to boost your mood? What will you do while commuting to work? How will you spend your leisure time?

The wisdom of *Groundhog Day* leads to a striking conclusion. You have the ability to transform your life day by day, and turn an ordinary day into an extraordinary one. But what would an extraordinary day look like? Do you envisage getting married? Lying on a tropical beach? Accepting an award at a dinner in your honour?

Phil proves that you do not need to wait for that perfect event or for fortune to move in your direction. You can create the perfect day by refining the way you experience your time. You have all the resources you need, and just have to learn how to use them. Your perfect day is about your state of mind and how you feel about yourself, about other people and about life in general. It is an inner experience of joy, peace and fulfilment that you can feel as you attend the dullest meeting, wait in the longest queue or search in vain for that one parking space!

If Phil can turn the worst day into the best day – so can you. All you need to do is engage with life, yourself and other people.

Your daily life is your temple and your religion.
Whenever you enter into it take with you your all.[87]
Kahlil Gibran, artist and poet

Even if not *every* day is amazing, you still have the ability to improve the overall quality of your experience by engaging fully with today. Now you have escaped the Groundhog Day Condition, learned to be present and appreciative, discovered the power of renewal and practice and found meaning and connection, you are ready to enjoy a great time more often – wherever you are and whatever you are doing.

leading a fully engaged life

Whenever you are feeling low, disappointed or frustrated, remember to engage. Let me offer you a simple three-step process that integrates the principles of this book:

1. **Engage with the present moment.** Slow down and stop what you are doing. Be still and quiet. Focus on your breathing for one minute, and breathe more slowly. Check that you are still and present.

2. **Engage with your Authentic Self.** While remaining quiet and present, consider your vision and your values. What is your purpose? What is the bigger picture in your life? What are you most passionate about? Check that you are being authentic.

251

3. **Engage with the world.** Now think of your loved ones, of your community and the wider world. Stop thinking about what you want and focus instead on how you are going to contribute to other people's lives. Check that you are being compassionate.

This simple practice helps you re-engage with what really matters in life. It interrupts negative patterns of doubt, worry and self-absorption and reconnects you back to your Authentic Self. Every time you reaffirm awareness, authenticity and compassion you are strengthening your capacity for a leading a rewarding life.

To break free from the Groundhog Day Condition, practise engagement again and again, and ensure that you consistently interrupt habitual patterns of thinking. You will need to be on guard all the time so you don't slip back into your Conditioned Self. Throughout today and every day stay engaged in everything you do.

Full engagement also requires that you follow the seven vital practices below, including appreciation, resilience, resourcefulness and agility which we looked at in Chapter Seven. When they are all present in everything you do, you will lead a happy and fulfilling life:

1. The practice of mindfulness
2. The practice of appreciation
3. The practice of living by your values
4. The practice of resilience

5. The practice of resourcefulness
6. The practice of agility
7. The practice of connection

Let's look at how you can apply each of these, embedding them into your daily routine.

MINDFULNESS

Mindfulness is the practice that supports all others as it interrupts your habitual thinking and behaviour, and creates a space for you to choose your thoughts and actions. Throughout the day be mindful of what you are thinking and feeling. Whenever you feel stressed or anxious, focus on your breathing and be aware of how you feel, what you hear and what you see.

Let's say you have been called into a meeting with your HR manager, and you assume that you're going to be issued with a warning or even made redundant. Let it go. Don't ruminate or catastrophise. You have no idea why they want to see you. It could even be about a promotion or pay rise. Remember that you are much more than your thoughts; they are fleeting, like clouds passing across the sky. Take three or four deep breaths to clear your head and move on to how you want to be spending your time. When you are calm and relaxed, you are far better placed to do your work and also enjoy your personal life.

APPRECIATION

The more you appreciate the simple pleasures of life, the happier you will be. From the moment you get up to the moment you go to sleep, try to savour every moment of your day. When you are in the dullest of meetings, ask yourself, 'What is good about this?' Keep on asking this question during each and every activity and encounter, however difficult they might be. Ask it as you struggle to complete a tough task, or have an uncomfortable conversation. When you do this consistently, you will start to shift your mindset and improve the quality of your moment-to-moment awareness.

Also take time to savour what you eat and what you drink: savour taking a walk and observing Nature; savour listening to music and reading a good book. And, above all, savour the people in your life and all the many gifts they give you.

LIVING BY YOUR VALUES

You may think that you are too busy and don't have much time to really think about values. Yet, your values will help you to become more engaged, more passionate and achieve your goals both at home and at work. They provide powerful direction and motivation to help you overcome challenges and setbacks.

Your values are the principles that determine your actions every day at work and at home like trust, integrity, fairness or quality. They act as a compass, providing direction to help you make better choices. Whenever you are faced with a challenge, like whether to have a difficult conversation with a colleague or not, or whether to cut corners to save time, it's important to be in tune with your values so you make the right decision. If you can think of a time when you didn't act in accordance with your values you'll know how damaging this can be, and how bad it can feel.

Values also give you meaning and fulfilment. If you are considering a new career or a change in lifestyle, this is particularly relevant. You may work primarily for money or career advancement at the moment, but if you can align your work with your values, you will flourish and be more successful in a much broader sense of the word. Think of those times in your life when you were part of something bigger – maybe a team, maybe your friends and family, maybe a community. Remember how great it was to align your values to what you were doing.

RESILIENCE

This is the skill of being mentally tough and bouncing back from adversity. Let's say you have been passed over for a promotion or feel a friend has rejected you. You have a choice of how to respond. Like Phil, decide on the optimal way of dealing with your predicament, accept what has happened and focus on taking action, not dwelling on how you feel.

Take personal responsibility and stop blaming others, or playing the victim. Every time you learn and grow from setbacks, you can turn what seems like failure into success. This makes you stronger and helps you stay engaged, optimistic and able to perform at your best over the long term.

RESOURCEFULNESS

Being resourceful means looking at what you do every day through fresh eyes, and being more effective at working with the resources available to you. Often, you already have what you need to find an innovative approach.

Resourceful people consistently challenge their mindset and their habits. They are always looking for creative ways to learn and improve, and often tend to be more successful and also happier, as they always see a way forward, and have a broader vision of what is possible.

Try making small adjustments to your daily routine, and let go of old habits that have not served you. Like Phil, when you learn to make the best of every situation, every challenge and every setback, you will make the most out of every day.

AGILITY

The world is changing rapidly and you will need to be agile to keep up. You need to embrace continuous change, even if you prefer the status quo. Consider how you can reinvent those aspects of your life that have kept you stuck. It may be in your working methods or in your relationships.

At work, do not stick rigidly to your formal roles and responsibilities. Instead, be constantly alert for new information, new ideas and new ways of doing things. Seize the initiative and take on new projects. Demonstrate that you are agile and open to new opportunities.

In your personal life try varying your routine and experimenting more. Go to new places and meet new people. Above all, be agile in your thinking. Catch yourself as you slip back into repetitive thoughts like, 'Why don't I have more interesting friends?' or, 'My life is going nowhere'. Instead, think new thoughts like, 'Where can I go today to meet a new group of people?' and, 'Who can I talk to who will help me be clearer about my goals?' Agile people focus their questions on taking action: planning what they are going to do next and then doing it.

CONNECTION

I teach a leadership style known as Transformational Leadership.[88] Think of all your interaction with other people as fitting into one of two categories: transactional' or 'transformational'.

You are 'transactional' when you treat relationships primarily as a transaction, a task to be completed and a means to an end. So, if you have to collaborate with a colleague to write a report, you are primarily interested in giving or receiving information. Their purpose is to serve your needs, and to help you complete the task.

You are transformational when you treat relationships primarily as an opportunity for growth. While working on the report, you seek to understand your colleague's needs and make a positive difference to them. You want to help them get what they want as well as what you want. You actively look for the good in people, and every conversation, every interaction provides an opportunity for you to build a strong relationship based on trust, openness and a mutual interest that might help to transform both parties' lives.

Phil shifted from being transactional to becoming transformational and so can you. Moreover, this is a wonderful way to work and live your life. It is not easy as it means leaving your ego behind and taking a risk. Some people may not reciprocate, and some may take advantage. You may feel let down or even rejected. But you know what? It does not matter. What matters is that you are being transformative. You are taking the initiative to build better relationships. And that way you become a far better team player, leader, friend, partner and parent.

the practice of happiness

Everything I have written so far is intended to contribute to one, overarching goal: I want to help you become happier. Happiness is much more than a temporary feeling that comes to you when things go your way. It is a state of mind that you can cultivate through practice.

At the beginning of *Groundhog Day* Phil was passive, waiting for the right circumstances for him to feel good. Then he took responsibility for his own wellbeing, and created the conditions to support it. He soon realised that seducing women and tricking people were fleeting pleasures, and began to develop habits that supported sustainable happiness. He had the perfect environment and all the time in the world to practise being happy. And so do you. Today is *the day*. You can choose to be happy or not. Remind yourself of this every morning.

Phil Connors undergoes a unique process that fundamentally alters his perception of himself and of his reality. You cannot recreate this exact process, but you can apply the most important elements to gain profound insight into how you should experience the rest of your life.

Imagine that you had an omniscient guide who could show you a hundred potential scenarios that were all available to you. Then imagine that one of these stood out, and inspired you far more than the others. Surely you would choose that scenario and do whatever it took to play it out?

Above all, focus on how you want to feel in the future. How will you feel at peace, happy and loved? Imagine savouring each moment of each day. Then try new experiences until you find a way of living that really satisfies your Authentic Self.

SUMMARY

- Work on each day, rather than your whole life. Because when you improve the quality of each day, you transform your life.

- With practice you can create your perfect day.

- Keep a daily journal to record your small improvements, which will accumulate into significant change.

- Learn to be a better decision maker: your quality of life is largely determined by the quality of the small decisions you make through the day.

- Think about what you would do if you had your time over again, and live that way today and every day.

- Learn how to master the quality as well as the quantity of your time.

- The key to mastering the art of living is to engage with life, with your authentic self and with the world.

living the wisdom of *Groundhog Day*

We are not provided with wisdom, we must discover it for ourselves, after a journey through the wilderness which no one else can take for us, an effort which no one can spare us.[89]

Marcel Proust, novelist and critic

Groundhog Day is a story of how a man discovers wisdom on a journey through the wilderness. He is lost in time and place, but finds the wisdom that was always present within him. You too have great wisdom within. Your wisdom is your ability to think and act from a deep sense of knowing and understanding, based on direct experience. It is sound judgment and penetrating insight. It is awareness of self and of what is happening around you. It is acting with integrity, and in accordance with your values. It is the admission that life is a mystery, the acknowledgment that everything is in flux and the flexibility to reinvent yourself continuously.

Wisdom is also a set of principles and practices that guide you in your thinking and action. A manual for life, if you like. These principles and practices are universal in that they are available to, and achievable by, everyone. You do not need a special talent, skill or qualification. They are authentic in terms of representing your values and who you are, rather than your Conditioned Self. They promote your physical and emotional wellbeing. They are ethical and are good for the wellbeing of others and the earth we live on. They are rational and evidence-based.

Before making decisions or taking action, I consistently ask myself these six questions:

- Is this achievable?
- Is it authentic, and what I really want?
- Is it good for me?
- Is it good for the other people concerned?
- Is it good for the wider world and the environment?
- Is it logical, based on common sense and evidence?

Answering these questions helps to keep me on the right track, and to be wiser. We also become wiser as we learn from the experience of engaging more fully with every aspect of our lives. You have this wisdom, and it just needs nurturing through practice.

Phil Connors gains wisdom through a continuous process of self-discovery, and by becoming more engaged to everything and everyone. At the outset he is disengaged, but gradually he engages with the pace of life, with his values and with other people. Above all, he engages with the natural resources that he already has: appreciation of the present moment, the gift of choice and the joy of unconditional love and connection.

The film is also a microcosm of a life in one day: being stuck in time represents a frame of reference that accentuates, and helps make sense of our development over a lifetime. You can see how hard it is to change. You can see that if you keep on repeating the same behaviours and acting from the same mindset, you will continue to get the same results.

As you watch Phil's character progress in the face of adversity, you can also see, in sharp relief, the contrast between a life built on awareness, gratitude, passion, compassion and service, and one built on ignorance, dissatisfaction, cynicism, self-interest and isolation.

In essence, the wisdom of *Groundhog Day* encourages you to recreate yourself: to evaluate your old conditioning and 'recondition' yourself by choice. You have the power to develop the qualities, values and habits that will serve you best. You can direct your own life. So choose the life you want – one that you will love each and every day.

Now it's over to you. What sort of future are you going to create for yourself? Are you going to be disengaged or engaged with life? Are you going to focus on improving your standard of living or your standard of experience?

You have the opportunity to embark on the most exciting and liberating journey of your lifetime. The journey within is more fascinating and inspiring than travelling the world. You can progress to new levels of consciousness, and write a new story about how you are going to live. As you engage with time, you learn from the past, savour the present and are optimistic about the future.

You are also coming home. Coming home is returning to your natural state of joy, love and wellbeing. When I watch *Groundhog Day* I see Punxsutawney as home. I feel a warm glow and a deep knowing that I cannot put into words. I yearn for the intimacy of the small town, the slow pace of life and the deep connection to place. I also know that I do not need to move again to find it. It is right here waiting for me. And it is waiting for you too. You just need to open your eyes and fully engage with life as it is. Like Phil, you can transform your life day by day, and be happy and fulfilled, here and now. This is genuine engagement. This is the wisdom of *Groundhog Day*.

glossary

authentic self

Your Authentic Self is the part of you that exists beyond your roles, responsibilities and personas. It is who you were before your conditioning from parenting, education and other influences; and it is the part of you that is calm, content and fulfilled, irrespective of your circumstances.

Your personal development is largely a process of shifting from your Conditioned Self to your Authentic Self.

conditioned self

Your Conditioned Self is the part you present to the outside world, and also to yourself. It is how you want others to think of you, and how you think you ought to be to achieve your goals. It is your personality built from your conditioning, going back to childhood. It tends to have strong needs like approval, control and entitlement. Your Conditioned Self always needs circumstances to be ideal to be happy, and is never satisfied.

doing and being modes

Throughout the day you are typically in doing mode – largely lost in thought or activities, operating on autopilot and disengaged from the world around you. In being mode, you are mindful of your experience from moment to moment. You are aware of your thoughts, but do not give them your full attention. You are simply present without the need to distract yourself by dwelling on the past or being preoccupied with the future.

engagement

Engagement is connecting to your life, to yourself and to the world. You are engaged with life when you are present and savour your time. You are disengaged when you are thinking about the past or future, and are busy rushing from one activity or task to the next.

You are engaged with yourself when you are self-aware – when you acknowledge your feelings and live by your values; you are disengaged when you are unaware of your patterns of thinking, your feelings and values. You are engaged with the world when you are loving, compassionate and serve others; you are disengaged when you are withdrawn, self-absorbed and lack purpose.

groundhog day condition

The Groundhog Day Condition is the feeling of being stuck in your own personal version of *Groundhog Day*. It can refer to the daily routines of your 'outer life', such as your work or relationships; and, more importantly, to the repetitions of your 'inner life', such as your thinking, feelings and habits. It is characterised by compulsive thoughts, a feeling of living on autopilot, a sense of meaninglessness and powerlessness to change.

personal reality

Your personal reality is how you see and interpret the world through the eyes of your Conditioned Self. It is your unique system of thoughts, attitudes, emotions and values. Your personal reality filters your perception and creates your experience.

quality time

Quality time is the moment-to-moment quality of your experience. It is your ability to be present and make the most of your time at work and at home. You can increase the quality of your time by changing your perception of time, being more mindful and learning to appreciate and savour each day, hour, minute and second of your precious time.

endnotes

1 Lennon, John, 'Instant Karma' (1970), Apple Records.

2 www.buddhism.about.com/od/abuddhistglossary/g/Samsaradef.htm.

3 Deikman, Arthur J., *The Observing Self* (1982), Free Press, p. 129.

4 Camus, Albert, *The Myth of Sisyphus* (1942), p. 489.

5 There is an excellent overview of the challenge of Employee Engagement here http://www.engageforsuccess.org/.

6 Dweck, Carol, *Mindset: The New Psychology of Success* (2006), Random House.

7 Seligman, M. E. P., Maier, S. F., 'Failure to escape traumatic shock' (1967), *Journal of Experimental Psychology*, 74: 1–9.

8 Freud, A., *The Ego and the Mechanisms of Defence* (1937), Hogarth Press and Institute of Psycho Analysis.

9 www.nimh.nih.gov/health/topics/generalized-anxiety-disorder-gad/index.shtml.

10 Dickens, Charles, *A Christmas Carol. In Prose. Being a Ghost Story of Christmas,* (1843), Chapman & Hall, p. 30.

11 Williamson, Marianne, *A Return to Love: Reflections on the Principles of "A Course in Miracles"* (1992), HarperOne.

12 Jonah Complex in Maslow, Abraham, *The Farther Reaches of Human Nature* (1971), Viking Press.

13 Neal, David T., Wood, Wendy and Quinn, Jeffrey M., 'Habits – A

Repeat Performance' (2006), *Current Directions in Psychological Science*, vol. 15, no.4.;
www.dornsifecms.usc.edu/assets/sites/208/docs/Neal.Wood.
Quinn.2006.pdf.

14 Duhigg, Charles, *The Power of Habit: Why We Do What We Do in Life and Business* (2012), Random House.

15 Fromm, Erich, *Sane Society* (1955), Routledge, p. 120, sect. C.2.b, 'Alienation'.

16 Thoreau, Henry David, *Walden; or, Life in the Woods* (1854), Ticknor and Fields: Boston.

17 Max-Neef, Manfred A. with Elizalde, Antonio, Hopenhayn, Martin, 'Human scale development: conception, application and further
reflections' (1989), New York: Apex.

18 Retrieved 14 July 2015 from http://www.brainyquote.com/quotes/quotes/w/wsomerset120765.html.

19 http://www.huffingtonpost.com/monique-honaman/groucho-marx-i-have-just-_b_800230.html.

20 'Enjoy Yourself', written by Carl Sigman and lyrics by Herb Magidson (1949)

21 Maslow, Abraham, *The Farther Readies of Human Nature* (1971), Viking Press, p. 25.

22 Seneca, *Penguin Great Ideas: On the Shortness of Life* (2004), Penguin.

23 Csikszentmihalyi, M., *Flow: The Psychology of Optimal Experience* (1990), Harper and Row.

24 www.psychologydictionary.org/contrast-effect/.

25 Kabat-Zinn, J., *Wherever you go, there you are: Mindfulness meditation in everyday life* (1994), New York: Hyperion, p. 4.

26 Lyubomirsky, S., Nolen-Hoeksema S., 'Effects of self-focused rumination on negative thinking and interpersonal problem solving' (1995), *Journal of Personality and Social Psychology*, 69(1), 176–90.

27 http://www.brainyquote.com/quotes/quotes/w/williamjam132270.html.

28 Schonert-Reichl, Kimberly A., Oberle, Eva, Stewart, Molly, Lawlor, David, Abbott, Thomson, Kimberly, Oberlander, Tim F. and Diamond, Adele, 'Enhancing Cognitive and Social–Emotional Development Through a Simple to Administer Mindfulness-Based School Program for Elementary School Children Psychology' (2015), *American Psychological Association*, vol. 51, no. 1, 52–66; Karelaia, Natalia and Reb, Jochen, *Improving Decision Making Through Mindfulness* (2014), Cambridge University Press.

29 Killingsworth, M. A., Gilbert, D. T. 'A Wandering Mind Is an Unhappy Mind' (2010), *Science*, vol. 330. no. 6006, p. 932, DOI: 10.1126/science.1192439.

30 http://www.wjh.harvard.edu/~dtg/KILLINGSWORTH%20&%20 GILBERT%20%282010%29.pdf.

31 http://www.brainyquote.com/quotes/quotes/b/blaisepasc133380.html.

32 Proust, Marcel, *Remembrance of Things Past* (1923), vol. V, *The Captive*.

33 Sendak, Maurice, *Higglety Pigglety Pop! Or, There Must Be More to Life* (1979), HarperCollins.

34 Dunn, Elizabeth and Norton, Michael, *Happy Money: The Science of Smarter Spending* (2013), Simon & Schuster.

35 Seligmain, Martin E. P., Steen, Tracy A., Park, Nansook and Peterson, Christopher, 'Positive Psychology Progress: Empirical Validation of Interventions' (2005), *American Psychologist*, 60(5), 410–21; Emmons, Robert A. and McCullough, Michael E., *The Psychology of Gratitude (Series in Affective Science)* (2004), Oxford University Press.

36 Kahneman, Daniel, *Thinking, Fast and Slow* (2011), Farrar, Straus and Giroux

37 Einstein quoted in Dellinger, David T., *From Yale to Jail : The Life Story of a Moral Dissenter* (1993), Pantheon Books.

38 http://visual.ly/what-are-odds.

39 Ware, Bronnie, *The Top Five Regrets of the Dying: A Life Transformed by the Dearly Departing* (2012), Hay House UK.

40 Keller, Helen, *Open Door* (1957), Doubleday.

41 Quoidbach, J., Berry, E. V., Hansenne, M. and Mikolajczak, M.,

'Positive Emotion Regulation And Well-being: Comparing The Impact Of Eight Savoring And Dampening Strategies' (2010), *Personality and Individual Differences,* 49(5), 368–73.

42 http://greatergood.berkeley.edu/expandinggratitude.

43 Elgin, Duane, *Voluntary Simplicity: Toward a Way of Life That is Outwardly Simple, Inwardly Rich* (1981), Morrow.

44 www.buddhanet.net/cbp2_f4.htm.

45 Ware, Bronnie, *The Top Five Regrets of the Dying: A Life Transformed by the Dearly Departing,* (2012), Hay House UK.

46 *Tree of Life* (2011), River Road Entertainment, Fox Searchlight Pictures.

47 Thayer, Robert E., *The Origin of Everyday Moods: Managing Energy, Tension, and Stress: Managing Energy, Tension and Stress* (1997), Oxford University Press, New Ed edition.

48 Brown, Brene, *Daring Greatly: How the Courage to Be Vulnerable Transforms the Way We Live, Love, Parent, and Lead* (2012), Gotham.

49 Peper, Erik and Lin, I-Mei, 'Increase or Decrease Depression: How Body Postures Influence Your Energy Level', *Association for Applied Psychophysiology & Biofeedback*, vol. 40, issue 3, pp. 125–30.

50 Frankl, Viktor E., *The Will to Meaning. Foundations and Applications of Logotherapy* (1988), New American Library, New York.

51 http://relationshipsinamerica.com/religion/are-religious-people-happier-people.

52 https://humanism.org.uk/about/our-aims/.

53 Maslow, Abraham, *The Farther Reaches of Human Nature* (1976), New York: Penguin. p. 36.

54 Jung, C. G., *Psychology and Religion: West and East, vol. 11, Collected Works* (1969), Princeton University Press.

55 Rand, Ayn, *For the New Intellectual* (1961), New York: Penguin.

56 www.psychologytoday.com/blog/two-takes-depression/201102/acceptance-and-commitment-therapy.

57 Shmotkin, D., 'Happiness in face of adversity: Reformulating the

dynamic and modular bases of subjective well-being' (2005), *Review of General Psychology*, 9, 291–325.

58 Miller, William R. and C'de Baca, Janet, *Quantum Change: When Epiphanies and Sudden Insights Transform Ordinary Lives* (2001), Guilford Press.

59 Haskins, Henry S., *Meditations in Wall Street* (1940), William Morrow & Co. (often misattributed to Ralph Waldo Emerson – see http://quoteinvestigator.com/2011/01/11/what-lies-within/).

60 Camus, Albert (translated from the French by Conroy Kennedy, Ellen), *Lyrical and Critical Essays* (1968), Knopf, p. 169.

61 Thoreau, Henry, *Walden; or, Life in the Woods* (1854), Ticknor and Fields: Boston, chapter 2, p. 15.

62 https://hbr.org/2010/06/are-you-a-high-potential.

63 Quoted in Albom, Mitch, *Tuesdays with Morrie* (1997), Doubleday.

64 'You'll Never Walk Alone', by Richard Rodgers and Oscar Hammerstein II from the musical *Carousel* (1945).

65 Maslow, Abraham, *Toward a Psychology of Being* (1962), Princeton, N.J.: D. Van Nostrand Co.

66 His Holiness the Dalai Lama and Cutler, Howard C., *The Art of Happiness* (1998), Riverhead Books.

67 'Charles M. Schulz Quotes', Quotes.net. STANDS4 LLC, 2015. Web. 10 Mar. 2015. < www.quotes.net/quote/54772>.

68 Leonard Cohen, interview in the *Observer*, 21 October 2001.

69 Boehm, J. K. and Lyubomirsky, S. (in press), 'The promise of Sustainable Happiness', in Lopez, S. J. (ed.), *Handbook of Positive Psychology* (2nd ed.) (2011), Oxford: Oxford University Press.

70 Peck, M. Scott, *The Road Less Travelled* (1978), Arrow Books.

71 http://www.alumni.nottingham.ac.uk/netcommunity/page.aspx ?pid=848.

72 Kelly, Bob, *Worth Repeating: More Than 5,000 Classic and Contemporary Quotes* (2003), Kregel Academic & Professional, p. 263.

73 Coleridge, Samuel Taylor, 'Work without Hope', http://www.poetryfoundation.org/poem/173255.

74 Erikson, E., *Childhood and Society* (1950), New York: Norton.

75 Calaprice, Alice, *The New Quotable Einstein* (2005) Princeton University Press, p. 206.

76 http://greatergood.berkeley.edu/topic/compassion.

77 Brian Cox in The Human Universe (2014), BBC; http://www.bbc.co.uk/programmes/p0276p50; https://en.wikipedia.org/wiki/Human _Universe.

78 Earth Charter – http://www.earthcharterinaction.org/invent/images /uploads/echarter_english.pdf.

79 Coué, Emile, *Self-Mastery Through Conscious Autosuggestion* (1922), 500 Fifth Avenue, New York.

80 *Gone with the Wind* (1939), Sidney Howard, Selznick International Pictures and Metro-Goldwyn-Mayer.

81 Gilbert, Daniel, *Stumbling on Happiness* (2006), Knopf.

82 *About Time*, Richard Curtis (2013), Working Title Films and Universal Pictures.

83 *Magic Eye: A New Way of Looking at the World* (1996), Magic Eye Inc. http://www.magiceye.com/.

84 *It's a Wonderful Life* (1946), Liberty Films and RKO Radio Pictures.

85 Frankl, Viktor E., *The Will to Meaning. Foundations and Applications of Logotherapy* (1988), New American Library, New York.

86 Nietzsche, Friedrich, *The Gay Science* (1882), translation, with commentary, by Kaufmann, Walter (1974), Vintage Books.

87 Gibran, Kahlil, *The Prophet* (1923), Knopf.

88 Bass, B. M. and Riggio, R. E., *Transformational Leadership* (2006), Routledge.

89 Proust, Marcel, *Remembrance of Things Past*, vol. II, 'Within a Budding Grove' (1924), Thomas Seltzer.

acknowledgments

I want to thank my colleague David Tully and my wife, Lorraine, for their invaluable feedback and suggestions. Many thanks to Liz Gough at Yellow Kite for publishing this book, and Emily Robertson and Anne Newman for their superb editing. Above all, I want to thank the late Harold Ramis and my friend Danny Rubin for making one of the greatest movies of all time. *Groundhog Day* has changed my life and I hope I can help many more people benefit from its profound wisdom.

books to help you live a good life

Join the conversation and tell
us how you live a #goodlife

🐦 @yellowkitebooks
📘 YellowKiteBooks
📌 Yellow Kite Books
📷 YellowKiteBooks